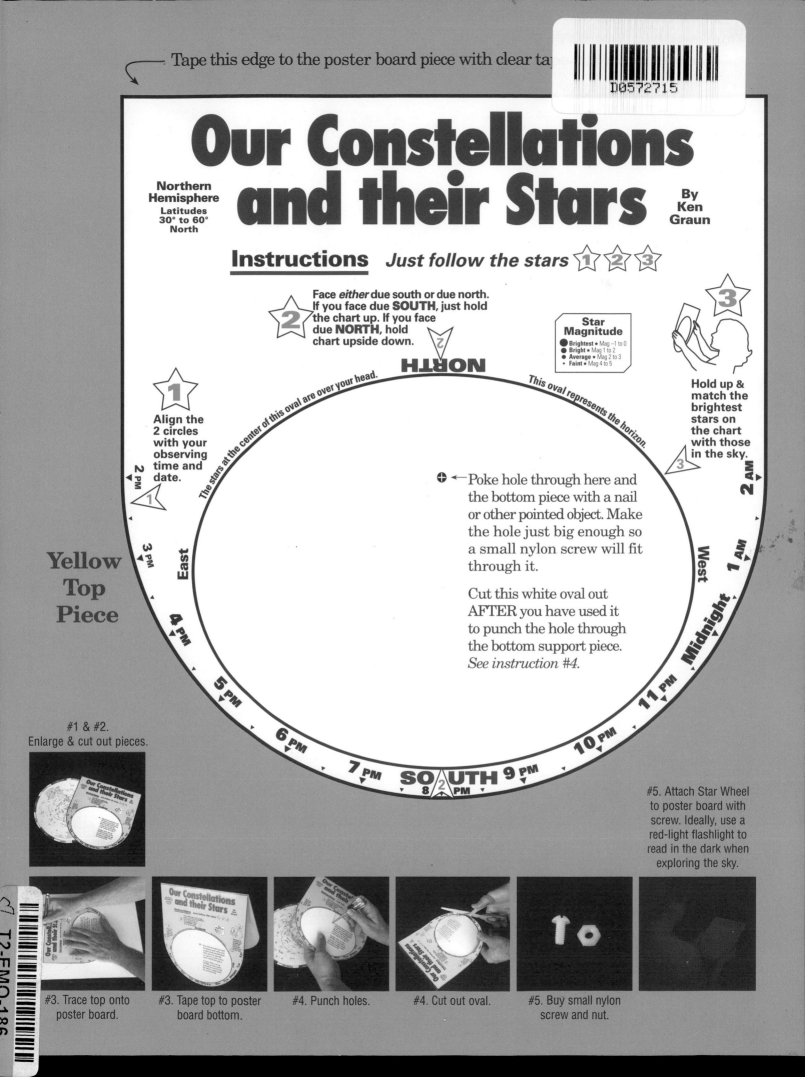

David H. Levy and Ken Graun

Ken Graun

is the author of the popular astronomy field guides, *Touring the Universe* and *What's Out Tonight?* He also coauthored, with David Levy, the beginner's star chart, *David H. Levy's Guide to the Stars. Our Constellations and their Stars* is his third book in the 21st Century Astronomy Series.

David H. Levy

has discovered 21 comets including Comet Shoemaker-Levy 9 that crashed into Jupiter in 1994. He is an Emmy award-winning writer and has written more than 30 astronomy books for children and adults. David is the science editor for the weekly *Parade* magazine.

Our Constellations
and their Stars

Ken Graun

Introduction by **David H. Levy**

Ken Press

The stars shine overhead to explore and enjoy. Have fun with them and share the joy of viewing them with others.
K. G.

Thw night sky is so inspiring and interesting. May this book help you to enjoy it as much as I have.
D. H. L.

Publisher's Cataloging-in-Publication

Graun, Ken.
  Our constellations and their stars / Ken Graun; introduction by
David H. Levy. — 1st ed. — Tucson, Ariz.: Ken Press, 2004.
    p. ; cm.
    (21st century astronomy series)

    Audience: grades 4–7.
    Includes index.
    SUMMARY: Introduces youngsters to the stars and
constellations. Includes star chart, distance and brightness
information for all major stars, and an expanded glossary.
    ISBN: 1-928771-09-2

    1. Constellations — Juvenile literature. 2. Stars—Juvenile literature.
  I. Title

QB802 .G73 2004   2003093148
523.8—dc21   0401

Published by Ken Press, Tucson, Arizona, United States of America ★ www.kenpress.com

Printed in Hong Kong by South Sea International Press Ltd

1 3 5 7 9 10 8 6 4 2

Introduction & Table of Contents

Top, from left:
Adrea Graun,
Sofia Lugo,
Anna Lugo,
Jimmy Broughton,
Sonya Lugo
and
Ryan Lindsey.

Bottom, from left:
Jasmine Council,
Sean Lindsey,
Jeremy Hibbs,
and
Elijah Hibbs.

A Key to the Heavens. Have you ever looked up at the stars and wondered about them? Asked yourself how many stars there are, how far away they are? Have you wondered how you can get to know them better? With this book your questions will be answered, but as you proceed, more questions will come to mind. That's the process of learning, and in the pages that follow you will begin to learn about the night sky.

I remember my first night viewing Jupiter and its moons with a small telescope. For me, that was a night of discovery. As you begin your own journey, you will make discoveries too. You will see constellations, the Moon, planets, meteors, and maybe a comet. They may even become friends to you, as they have for me. May this book help you enjoy your nights under the stars.

David H. Levy
June 25, 2003

SPECIAL NOTE on the names of CONSTELLATIONS and *Stars* used in this book. All constellation names are in UPPER CASE and the names of stars, including our *Sun*, are in *Italics*. There are also other words that are in italics for emphasis.

Stars in the Sky

When you look up into the night sky, you see pinpoints of light that we call stars. For the longest time, no one knew what they were. In fact, some ancient cultures thought they might be candles or fires resting on the inside of a giant ball.

It took the invention of the telescope around 1690 to bring understanding to the true nature of these tiny lights. As scientists studied the stars, they slowly discovered that they were faraway suns, that is, the stars were like our *Sun*, just as big and bright but very far away. It is only their great distances from us that makes them appear as pinpoints of light. If our *Sun* was moved to the distances of even the closer stars, its brightness would fade to one of the fainter stars in the night sky.

Nighttime & daytime stars

Did you know that the stars are out during the daytime? However, you cannot normally see them because the bright light from our *Sun* is scattered by our atmosphere, making the whole daytime sky light up and wash out the stars. It is possible, however, to see the brightest stars through a telescope during the day if you know where to look.

Where do the stars come from?

Every star, including our *Sun* formed inside a giant cloud of hydrogen gas called a nebula. The stars condense out of these hydrogen clouds in space similar to rain drops condensing out of the clouds in our atmosphere. The energy of stars, some of which we see as light, is produced from nuclear reactions occurring at their cores where there is tremendous pressure and heat.

It can easily take a million or so years for a new star to form in a hydrogen cloud. Depending on a new star's starting size, it can last anywhere from just a few million years to billions of years. Stars the size of our *Sun* last about 10 billion years. Our *Sun* is about 4½ billion years old.

Normal sizes of stars

Although our *Sun* is an average-sized star, the sizes of *normal* stars range from about 1/10 to 40 times its diameter. Since the diameter of our *Sun* is 865,000 miles, the smallest *normal* stars would therefore have diameters around 87,000 miles while the largest *normal* stars would have diameters that stretch to 35,000,000 miles. There are *much* smaller and larger stars than these but they are in a special class of stars whose lives are ending.

Brightness of stars

The stars in the sky vary in brightness for two reasons. The first is because they are all at different distances. The farther away a star is, the fainter it will appear. The second reason has to do with their sizes. Larger stars have more surface area so they give off more light and appear brighter than smaller stars. So, the brightness of stars vary because of a combination of their size and distance from us.

Twinkling

Stars twinkle because of air movement in our atmosphere. When pockets of air move about, they act like lenses and prisms, bending and spreading light a little, causing a star's light to slightly but briefly change direction, brightness and color. Stars twinkle more when they are closer to the horizon because you are looking through more atmosphere and more pockets of moving air.

Colors

At first glance, all the stars might appear white, but if you look at them a little closer you will notice that some have color. Red is the easiest color to see, but you may also be able to discern orange, yellow and blue. The colors appear best through a telescope. The temperature of the outer gaseous layer of a star determines its color. Red stars have cooler surfaces than blue and white stars. Our *Sun* is yellowish with a surface temperature of 10,000° F.

A galaxy of stars

Our *Sun* and all of the stars that you see in the night sky are located in a galaxy that we call the Milky Way Galaxy. A galaxy is a grouping of billions of stars. Our *Sun* is just one star among 100 billion that make up our Milky Way Galaxy. Our Milky Way Galaxy is just one galaxy of about 125 billion in the Universe.

Magnitude of Stars

Long ago, when the ancients looked up and studied the stars, they classified them by their brightness. We still use this same system of **magnitudes** today, however, we now have instruments to accurately measure a star's brightness. The range of magnitudes varies from –27 (spoken as "minus twenty-seven" or "negative twenty-seven") for the *Sun* to over +30 (spoken as "thirty," "plus thirty" or "positive thirty") for the faintest stars. Ask a parent or teacher about negative numbers.

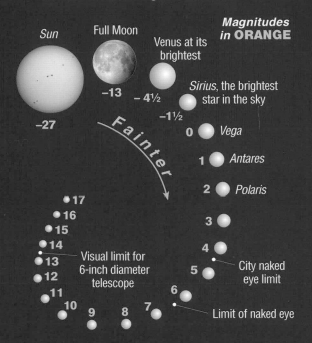

Magnitudes in ORANGE

Sun –27

Full Moon –13

Venus at its brightest –4½

Sirius, the brightest star in the sky –1½

Fainter

0 *Vega*

1 *Antares*

2 *Polaris*

3

4

5 — City naked eye limit

6 — Limit of naked eye

• 17
• 16
• 15
• 14
• 13 — Visual limit for 6-inch diameter telescope
• 12
• 11
• 10 9 8 7

This is part of the Eagle Nebula that resides within the boundaries of the constellation SERPENS (see page 20). Stars form inside giant hydrogen clouds like this. The arrows point to little fingers. Inside, stars are forming, condensing out of the hydrogen gas much like rain condenses out of water clouds. The width of these fingers have diameters 200 times greater than our solar system.

Our *Sun* is just one star in a galaxy that contains about 100 billion stars. Here is a galaxy that looks like our Milky Way Galaxy. This type of galaxy is called a spiral galaxy because it has arms that spiral or curve outward from a bulging center. The letter S marks where our *Sun* would be located if this were our galaxy.

Number of stars visible to magnitude...

Magnitude	Number of stars
5	is 2,800
6	is 8,700
7	is 27,000
8	is 78,000
9	is 218,000
10	is 586,000
11	is 1,000,000

MAGNITUDE FACTS

1 Each magnitude is about 2½ times brighter or fainter than the next magnitude.

2 The *Hubble Space Telescope*, in orbit about Earth, can record to magnitudes fainter than 30.

3 The magnitude of stars do not indicate their true brightness in comparison to the Sun.

Magnitudes of 10 brightest *Stars* & CONSTELLATIONS where they are located

Star	Constellation	Magnitude
Sirius	in CANIS MAJOR	–1½
Canopus	in CARINA	–½
Rigil Kent	in CENTAURUS	–¼
Arcturus	in BOOTES	0
Vega	in LYRA	0
Capella	in AURIGA	0
Rigel	in ORION	0
Procyon	in CANIS MINOR	½
Achernar	in ERIDANUS	½
Betelgeuse	in ORION	½

Well, the stars do move a little.

In this chapter and through-out this book, it is stated that the stars don't move and are fixed in the sky. This is how astronomers look upon the stars for everyday use.

However, all stars including our *Sun* are moving through space. Individually the stars are moving quite fast but because they are very far from one other, they appear to be moving extremely slow. You have experienced this same effect when driving down a freeway. The more distant cars appear to be mov-ing slower than those nearby even though all the cars are traveling at about the same speed. The Moon, which is the closest celestial body to Earth, appears to be standing

The Big Dipper today.

The Big Dipper 100,000 years from now.

still even though it is moving around the Earth at 3,300 miles an hour.

This very slow movement of the stars is called "proper motion," and over very long periods of time will cause the shapes of the constella-tions to change.

The stars move because, like our *Sun*, they are all revolving around the center of our Milky Way Galaxy. It takes the *Sun* over 200 million years to complete a revolution about our galaxy's center.

To the left is an example of what the Big Dipper will look like in the far future.

It *does* feel as though the Earth is standing still.

We cannot feel the Earth turning even though those living at the equator are moving over 1,000 miles per hour compared to someone at the pole who merely turns in a circle.

Why don't we feel the Earth spinning daily on its axis? Simply because this motion is constant and smooth. It is the same reason we don't sense any "speed" when we are in a plane or car (but we do feel all the bumps and turns which are not part of the constant, smooth motion). The ancients thought the Earth stood still because it does feel like it is not moving. However, if you are at the equator, you are moving around Earth's circumference at 1,038 miles per hour. If you are at a pole, you don't move, you just rotate in a circle once every 24 hours. Now get this, *everyone* on Earth is moving around the *Sun* at 67,000 miles per hour but we don't feel it because this speed is also constant.

6

Moving Moon

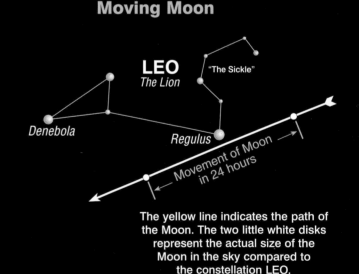

The yellow line indicates the path of the Moon. The two little white disks represent the actual size of the Moon in the sky compared to the constellation LEO.

The Moon is *the* closest celestial body to Earth and orbits our planet every 29 days (New Moon to New Moon). At this rate of revolution, it moves through the sky 12 arc degrees (see Glossary) eastward from night to night, which is equivalent to the length of 24 Moons lined up side by side. Watch the Moon from night to night and observe its journey through the stars.

Movements in the Sky

The *Sun* moves across the sky during the day while the stars and Moon move through it at night. Both of these movements occur because the Earth spins or rotates on its axis once a day.

You may also have noticed or been told that the stars in the summer night sky are not the same as those in the winter night sky. If you have not noticed this, then you probably have observed that the *Sun* is much higher in the summer sky at noon than during winter. These changes happen because the Earth orbits or revolves around the *Sun* once a year.

Daily rotation

The Earth spins on its axis counterclockwise once a day. The axis is an imaginary line that passes through both the north and south poles. Any spinning object has an axis that it rotates about. Spin a small object and you will see that there is a center point around which the rest of the body rotates. This center point is on the axis of the spinning object just like the poles are on the axis of the rotating Earth.

The most noticeable effect of the Earth's rotation is the daily rising and setting of the Sun, Moon and stars. These objects rise in the east and set in the west because the Earth rotates counterclockwise on its axis. The only place on Earth where the stars don't rise or set is at the poles. Here, they just circle around a point in the sky directly overhead. The stars near the horizon move in large circles around the sky while those closest to the top of the sky move in smaller circles.

Yearly revolution

Each day, the Earth makes a complete turn on its axis, but it takes one year for the Earth to orbit the *Sun*, that is, to revolve or circle around it. As the Earth orbits the *Sun*, the night side faces different directions in space,

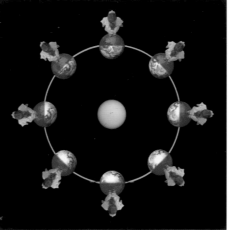

The reason that we see different constellations throughout the year is because the Earth's night side faces different directions.

which allows us to see different sets of constellations over a year's time. It takes about one month to notice some new stars rising in the east and about five months to see an entire new set of stars in the evening sky.

Now you may think, "If the Earth turns completely around once a day, shouldn't we see all the stars in a day's time?" The answer to this question would be yes if it were not for the brightness of the sky during the day.

Stars so still

For all practical purposes, the stars in the sky do not move. You can think of them as pinholes in a giant ball that we call the "celestial sphere." Even though the Earth turns on its axis daily and circles the Sun yearly, the stars don't move. They only appear to move and change in the sky because of the Earth's turning and circling. Think of the stars as the pictures and nicknacks on the walls of your house. No matter how you turn or move about the house, the pictures and nicknacks stay in place.

Moon

Except for the *Sun*, the Moon is the most noticeable object in the sky. It is also the closest celestial body to the Earth and the only natural object to orbit our planet. The Moon circles the Earth counterclockwise about every 29 days, close to a month's time. This rate and direction of movement makes the Moon rise in the east about 50 minutes later each day.

The phases of the Moon are nothing more than seeing part of its night side and day side at the same time. Remember, the Earth, as well as all the other planets and their moons, always have a night side and day side. Why do you think this is so? The Moon's phases change because we see the Moon from different angles as it circles the Earth over a month's time.

The North Star

The North Star refers to the star named *Polaris* in the constellation URSA MINOR. *Polaris* is the bright end star that makes up the handle of a group of stars we call the Little Dipper. Several of the stars that make up the Little Dipper are very faint, so the whole Little Dipper is hard to see unless you live where the skies are very dark. *Polaris* is called the North Star because if you face it, you are facing north, no matter where you are on Earth.

Always points north

If you could look down on the Earth as it revolves yearly around the *Sun*, you would notice that the Earth's north pole always points in the same direction, which is close to the star *Polaris*. Why is this? As the Earth rotates daily on its axis, it acts like a gyroscope. All spinning objects act like a gyroscope. One of the natural properties of a gyroscope is that its spinning axis always points in the same direction, even if the gyroscope is moved about, or orbits around the Sun, as is the case with Earth.

Polaris, the star

Polaris stands out as a fairly bright star in the northern sky but it is not the brightest star. This second magnitude star is a little brighter than most stars and overall it is the 46th brightest star in the sky. Also, the axis of the Earth does not exactly point to *Polaris*. *Polaris* is a little less than the Moon's diameter from the true north point, the north celestial pole.

Polaris is 431 light years away (each light year is about 6 trillion miles) and is classified as a giant star because it is large, bright and "elderly." The diameters of elderly type stars

often are greater than normal because they bloat up as their hydrogen fuel is depleted. Compared to the *Sun*, *Polaris* has a diameter 60 times greater and it shines 3,600 times brighter. An interesting fact about *Polaris'* brightness is that it varies slightly every four days, but the change is too small to be noticed with the eyes. This change in brightness happens to many elderly stars. Our *Sun* is middle aged and will be around for billions of years.

North stars

Generally, only the brightest stars have names. However, there are exceptions.

In the constellation DRACO, which wraps around the Little Dipper, there is a rather faint star that has been given the name *Thuban* (see star chart on page 16). *Thuban* shines a little brighter than magnitude 4, which makes it five times fainter than *Polaris*. It was given a name because at one time, it *was* the North Star, just like *Polaris* is today. *Thuban* was the North Star 4,800 years ago when the Egyptians were still building pyramids. Since that time, the direction that the Earth's axis is pointing has slowly changed toward *Polaris*.

Precession

Toy tops act like little gyroscopes and when they slow down, they start to wobble in a circle. This wobbling is caused by gravity tugging on the top, trying to bring it down. The spinning Earth also gets tugged on by a combination of the *Sun's* and Moon's gravity. This causes it to wobble similarly to a slowing top. However, the Earth's wobble, known as precession, is very slow, taking 25,800 years to complete a circle.

BIG DIPPER'S END STARS POINT TO NORTH STAR

Polaris
"The North Star"

Little Dipper

Kochab
Pherkad

Dubhe   Merak
Big Dipper
Phad
Megrez
Alioth
Mizar
Alkaid

The Big Dipper is easy to find in the northern sky because the stars that make up its pattern are bright. If you can find the Big Dipper, then identifying *Polaris,* the North Star, is just a matter of following the two end stars of its bowl. All the stars in this illustration are sized to show their actual brightness — the bigger, the brighter. The Big Dipper is positioned as it appears in the early evening sky during late winter.

Although this movement may seem like it would be unnoticeable, it was known by the ancient Egyptians because they took accurate measurements of where stars rose and set over hundreds and thousands of years.

The effect of precession is that the Earth's poles point to different directions in the sky over the course of the 25,800 years wobble. During this lengthy period of time, the poles describe circular paths through the constellations. The poles will appear to point to any star along these paths but most of the time they will point to spots without stars.

No South Star

Polaris is only visible from the northern hemisphere. Thus, it cannot be seen south of the equator because it is blocked by the ground or Earth.

So, how do you find your direction at night if you are in Australia, southern South America or southern Africa? It is difficult at these locations to use the stars because there is no South Star in the southern hemisphere to help you orientate yourself. In fact, there is not even a fairly bright star close to the south celestial pole, which is the point in the sky that the south pole points to. Your best bet is to use a compass.

Toy gyroscopes are fun to play with and their motion demonstrates how the Earth's axis can stay tilted at the same angle.

Precession may be difficult to comprehend because it takes so long for Earth's axis to "wobble" the giant circles it makes in the sky. The orange-dotted line shows the northern hemisphere circle (there is another one for the southern hemisphere), which is the path that the north pole points to over the 25,800 years that it takes to complete a whole wobble. We are fortunate that we live during a time in history when the Earth's north pole points to a star. As you can see, most of the time, the Earth's north pole does not point to any star.

This picture was taken by pointing a camera north and keeping the shutter open for 15 minutes. *Polaris* is indicated by the arrow. All the other stars appear to revolve around *Polaris* because the Earth's axis points to it, giving the illusion that the other stars revolve around this center point. The star-streaks would have become longer if the shutter had been left open longer. Some of the leaves of the trees are white because a light was shining on them.

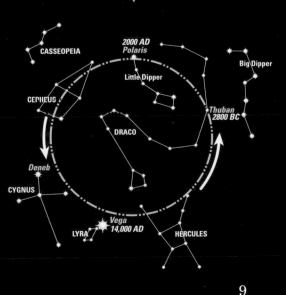

Constellations

There are a total of 88 constellations in the whole sky. These are listed at the back of this book. About 70 of them can be seen from the United States. The remaining have to be viewed from the southern hemisphere. Most of the northern hemisphere constellations that are recognized today were originally fashioned by the ancient Greeks and other cultures over two thousand years ago.

Borders

In these modern times, a constellation is actually a bordered area in the sky just like a state is defined by its borders. The borders of constellations were constructed to take into account their classical shapes. A star or object is said to be "in" a constellation when it is within its borders.

Beliefs, stories and mythology

We live at a time in history and in a culture that has a good scientific understanding of the world around us. Because of this, it is sometimes difficult to understand the beliefs of ancient cultures. During those times, starting thousands of years ago, people did not understand the workings of nature, so they made up stories to explain many natural events. This includes stories about thunder and lightning, the daily movement of the *Sun*, the wind and waves, and even the shapes of mountains. Often these stories involved mighty characters or gods who had the power to yield or create the wind, lightning and thunder. Over time, these stories became traditions, beliefs and even religions. This happened all over the world, with every culture from Europe to Africa and Asia on to the Americas. Each had its own stories to explain the workings of the world.

Now, the stars and everything else that appeared in the sky were also a mysterious part of nature, so many cultures incorporated these objects into their stories. Those stories that survived and influenced our culture the most were from the Greeks and Romans. Most people enjoy these mythological stories because they are entertaining and offer insights into human behavior. A good beginning book on mythology, one with wonderful illustrations is Ingri and Edgar Parin D'Aulaire's *Book of Greek Myths*. However, to get you started, a little mythology is provided with the star charts on pages 16 to 27.

Mythological thinking

Stories have a beginning, middle and end. Also, the events in stories unfold in a way that is believable and logical. Mythological stories can be different. Unlike most stories written today, these tales often take unusual twists and turns. One reason that this happens is because the ancient Greeks had a different outlook on life compared to what we have today.

All of the earliest celestial charts showed mythological characters. This set of four by Ignace Pardies of Paris was published in 1708 and is considered one of the best examples of the first charts. All the black lines and outlines were engraved in wood, which was used to print the

Continues on page 11

Shape and figures

For the most part, the patterns of stars that make up the constellations do not resemble their mythological figures. This is because the drawings for most of the mythological figures had to be forced to fit the stars in the sky.

Almagest

One of the oldest surviving astronomy books that includes a star atlas is titled, *Almagest*, meaning The Greatest. It was written by an Egyptian scholar named Ptolemy who lived around A.D. 150. This atlas has no star charts like those in this book but instead describes the location of the brighter stars in relationship to the parts that make up the mythological figures. For example, the location of *Aldebaran*, the bright red star in TAURUS, is described as the eye of the bull.

Names of stars

Most stars are not named. Only the brighter stars have names as well as other stars having special significance. Many of the names used today were originally given

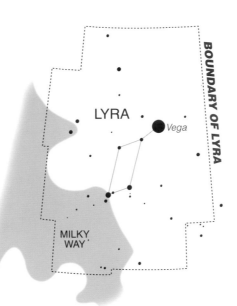

Each of the constellations in the sky has boundaries. These were constructed by modern astronomers to help identify the location of stars and other objects in the sky.

by the Arabs and Greeks several thousand years ago.

Celestial sphere

The ancient cultures thought the stars were affixed to the inside of a giant sphere that they called the Celestial Sphere. We still use this term today to indicate the realm or place where the stars reside. Additionally, the idea that the stars are affixed to a sphere is handy for, like globes made of the Earth, it provides a surface to indicate positions and boundaries, and to draw paths.

Stars whose names came from the Arabs

Aldebaran in **TAURUS** means "the follower of the Pleiades."
Alpheratz in **PEGASUS** means "horse's navel."
Antares in **SCORPIUS** means "rival of Mars" or "glowing redly."
Betelgeuse in **ORION** means "armpit," "shoulder" or "arm."
Deneb in **CYGNUS** means "hen's tail."
Rigel in **ORION** means the "left leg."

Stars whose names came from the Greeks

Arcturus in **BOOTES** means the "bear watcher" or "bear guard."
Canopus in **CARINA** means "rudder."
Capella in **AURIGA** means the "little she-goat."
Polaris in **URSA MINOR** means the "pole star."
Regulus in **LEO** means the "king," "mighty" or "great."
Sirius in **CANIS MAJOR** means "sparkling" or "scorching."
Spica in **VIRGO** means the "ear of wheat."

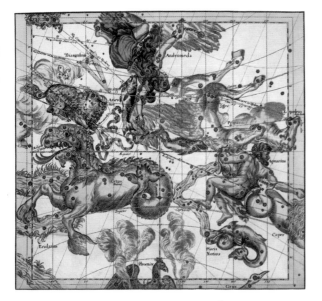

Continued from page 10

pages. The coloring was hand painted, one page at a time. Charts like this were often used for reference when studying the heavens and plotting the path of comets. An enlargement of TAURUS the Bull, shown to the immediate left, is featured on the front cover.

This star chart, from the early 1700s, was drawn by Johann Doppelmayr, a German mathematician. It is a little different in that it places the constellations of the zodiac along its circumference. This shifts the North Star, *Polaris* away from the center. Can you find it? Clue: Use the suggestion for finding *Polaris* on page 8.

Clue: Use the suggestion for finding *Polaris* on page 8.

CONSTELLATIONS OF THE ZODIAC

The ancients thought the constellations of the zodiac were special so each was given its own symbol. The zodiacal constellations are listed below in the order the *Sun* moves through them during the course of a year, starting with PISCES which is where the *Sun* is located at the start of spring.

PISCES
the
Fishes

ARIES
the
Ram

TAURUS
the
Bull

GEMINI
the
Twins

CANCER
the
Crab

LEO
the
Lion

VIRGO
the
Maiden

LIBRA
the
Scales

SCORPIUS
the
Scorpion

SAGITTARIUS
the
Archer

CAPRICORNUS
the
Sea Goat

AQUARIUS
the
Water Bearer

The ecliptic, or path of the *Sun,* is tilted 23½ degrees to the Earth's equator (indicated by the pink lines) because the Earth's axis is tilted 23½ degrees toward the plane of its orbit. The plane of Earth's orbit thus defines the ecliptic.

23½° Tilt

Axis

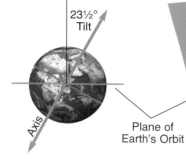

23½°
Tilt

Axis

Plane of
Earth's Orbit

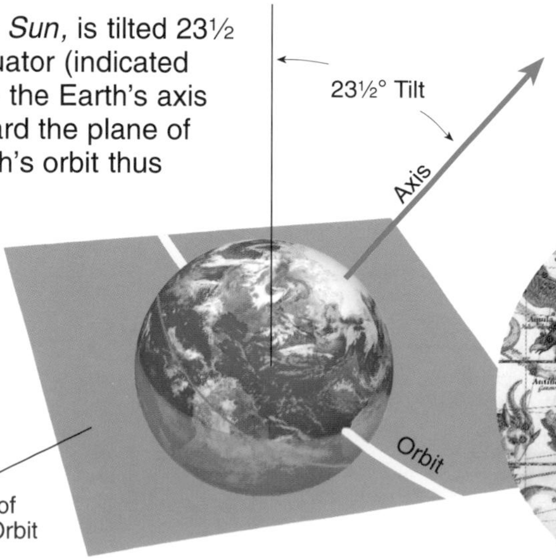

Orbit

OPHIUCHUS is the 13th constellation of the zodiac. As you can see from this 1720 chart, the Doctor's left leg dips between SAGITTARIUS and SCORPIUS, crossing the ecliptic as indicated by the red arrow.

The Zodiac

The zodiac is a band of 12 constellations that circle the sky. Almost everyone can name several, but which ones are they and what makes them special?

The constellations of the zodiac are listed to the left. These constellations became special thousands of years ago when the ancients realized that the *Sun* travels through them over the course of a year. However, today, in our modern era, there is no scientific value or special interest in these constellations even though the *Sun* passes through them.

Ecliptic

Each day the *Sun* appears to circle the sky because the Earth rotates on it axis. Each year the *Sun* appears to move through the 12 constellations of the zodiac completing another circle in the sky because the Earth orbits the *Sun*.

If, during the day, you could see the stars immediately around the *Sun*, the *Sun*'s position would always be located in one of the constellations of the zodiac. And, as the days passed, you would further notice the *Sun* slowly advancing eastward through the constellations of the zodiac, eventually completing a circle in the sky over a year's time. This yearly path or circle made by the *Sun* is called the ecliptic.

It is important to remember that the *Sun* does not actually move through these constellations. It is the Earth's yearly orbit around the *Sun* that creates the appearance the *Sun* moves among the stars.

Unfortunately, we cannot see the stars during the daytime. This is because the air in our atmosphere scatters so much of the *Sun*'s light, it makes the daytime sky brighter than any star, so it is not obvious which constellation the *Sun* is in or which ones it moves through.

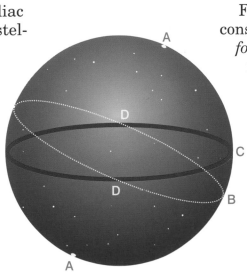

The blue sphere represents the celestial sphere where the stars "reside." The A's indicate the celestial poles, the spots where Earth's axis point to. B is the celestial equator which is the projection of Earth's equator. C is the ecliptic or plane of Earth's orbit (also see ecliptic on star charts). The constellations along C are the constellations of the zodiac. The D's, where the ecliptic and equator cross, are the vernal and autumnal equinoxes.

Twelve or thirteen

For thousands of years, the zodiac consisted of just 12 constellations, *one for each month of the year.* However, in modern astronomy, constellations have boundaries so there are actually 13 constellations that the path of the *Sun* or ecliptic passes through. The 13th is the constellation OPHIUCHUS, known as the Doctor or Serpent Bearer, and is positioned between SAGITTARIUS and SCORPIUS. It does not matter in astronomy whether there are 12 or 13 constellations of the zodiac because, again, these constellations have no special scientific significance or interest.

Astronomy and astrology

The zodiac conjures up astrology, superstious beliefs that began over 500 years ago.

Many people get astronomy and astrology confused. Astronomy is a science that studies everything outside our atmosphere. This means that objects like the *Sun*, Moon, planets and stars are examined with instruments such as telescopes to measure characteristics like size, distance, composition and temperature.

Astrology is not a science! It is a non-scientific interpretation of information that tries to predict events in our lives based on the position of the planets, Moon, *Sun* and stars. These predictions are written as horoscopes, which are often found in newspapers. *Predictions based on astrology are not true. Many scientists have studied horoscopes and have found that they do not predict events in our lives any better than guessing does.* So if you like reading horoscopes, have fun with them but don't take them seriously.

The Milky Way Band

Stretching through the stars, across the entire celestial sphere, is a faint glowing jagged band. If you live where the skies are dark, like in the country, you can easily see this milky path. However, you generally cannot see it from cities because all the outdoor lights make the night sky brighter than the Milky Way Band itself, washing it away.

What exactly is this band?

All of the stars that we see in the sky, from the faintest to the brightest are visible to the naked eye because they are fairly close. Stars that are farther away cannot be seen as pinpoints of light anymore; they can only appear to the eyes as faint glows. So, when you look at the Milky Way Band, you are actually seeing the faint glow from millions and millions of stars that are too distant and faint to see with your eyes individually. The stars that make up the Milky Way Band range from about 100 to 10,000 times farther away than those we can see with our eyes. There are about 100 billion stars along the Milky Way Band.

One question that may immediately pop into your mind is, "Why are there so many stars concentrated along this band instead of being spread evenly throughout the sky?" See the hula-hoop picture on the next page for the answer.

Thick and thin

The Milky Way Band is 66 Moon widths at its widest near SAGITTARIUS but narrows down to just 4 Moon widths by PERSEUS. The brightest part is where it is widest, between the constellations SAGITTARIUS and SCORPIUS. This area contains the highest concentration of stars because it is in the direction to the bulged center and core of our galaxy.

The thickest and brightest part of the Milky Way Band lies between SAGITTARIUS and SCORPIUS. This area can be observed during the early evenings of late summer. It comes up out of the southern horizon and then stretches overhead. The orange arrow points to the star *Kaus Borealis* and the pink arrow to *Kaus Media* in SAGITTARIUS (compare to chart on page 20). The green "+" sign indicates the direction to the core of our galaxy. The small pink spots are nebulae where stars are being born. The bright one indicated by the blue arrow is called the Lagoon Nebula.

From River to Band to Galaxy

For much of history, the Milky Way Band was considered the "River of Heaven." Many cultures believed that the Milky Way was the road departed souls took to their final resting place. Some Native Americans thought that the brightest stars on the Milky Way were campfires where souls rested on their journey.

Among the Arabs, the Milky Way was known simply as the "River." The Israelites called it the "River of

Light." In China and Japan, it was the "Silver River."

One of the earliest references to the appearance of the band being described as "milky" was in a hymn written around 800 B.C. by the famous Greek writer Homer who wrote the *The Iliad*, which is still read today. Later on, in Rome, it was thought of as the "Heavenly Girdle." Ptolemy, a great astronomer living around A.D. 150 labeled it the "Circle of the Milky Way" in his book, *Almagest*. By the middle ages, which is the period of history from about A.D. 500 to 1500, the term Milky Way was in common use.

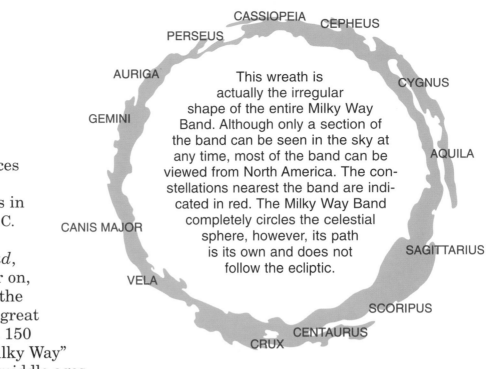

This wreath is actually the irregular shape of the entire Milky Way Band. Although only a section of the band can be seen in the sky at any time, most of the band can be viewed from North America. The constellations nearest the band are indicated in red. The Milky Way Band completely circles the celestial sphere, however, its path is its own and does not follow the ecliptic.

CASSIOPEIA CEPHEUS
PERSEUS
AURIGA   CYGNUS
GEMINI   AQUILA
CANIS MAJOR   SAGITTARIUS
VELA
SCORIPUS
CENTAURUS
CRUX

This is what the Milky Way Band looks like when you stretch it out. Notice that it is long, flattish and has a bulged center, which is the core of our galaxy. Astronomers have found this same shape in other galaxies throughout the Universe.

About 100 years ago, and after years of studying the heavens, astronomers concluded that the Milky Way Band did indeed represent the faint glow coming from the bulk of stars that make up our galaxy. When astronomers discovered this fact, they continued to use the name that our galaxy had unknowningly been called for centuries.

Follow the star charts

The star charts on the following pages indicate the path and shape of the Milky Way Band through the sky and should help you find it in your exploration of the stars.

Try This

Find the Milky Way Band using the star charts in this book. Observe it with binoculars, taking some time to explore and enjoy what you see. Now look at an area away from the Milky Way. Where do you see more stars?

Why is the Milky Way a band? The Milky Way appears as a band because the stars in our galaxy are arranged in the shape of a flat dish. The effect of seeing the Milky Way as a band is much the same as looking out from inside of a hulu-hoop. In this picture, Adrea's head is placed inside the plane of the hoop, which is where most of the stars, including our *Sun* are located. The hoop would represents the glow from all the stars that make up our galaxy.

North Circumpolar Stars

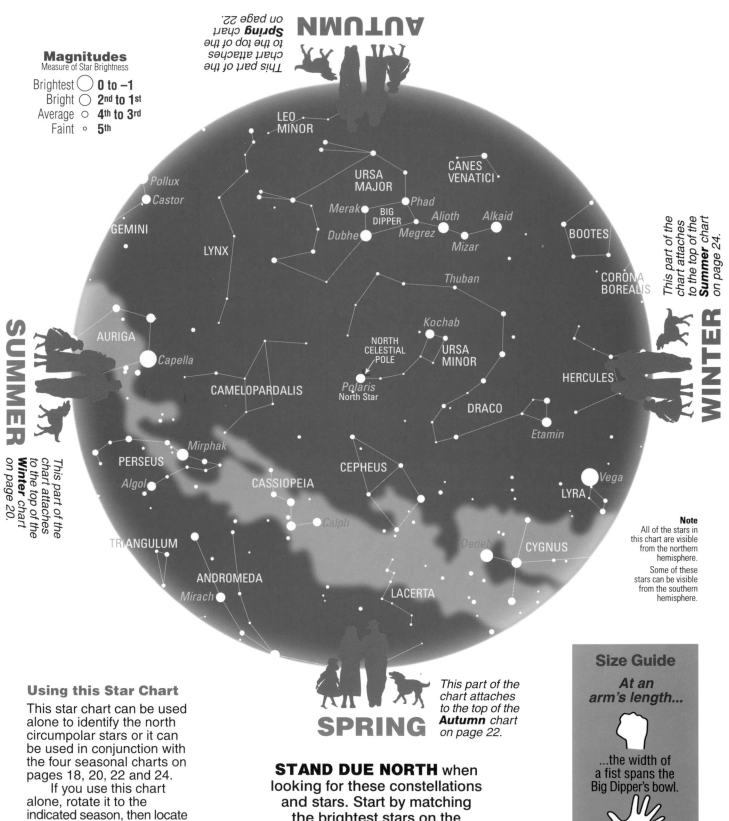

AUTUMN
This part of the chart attaches to the top of the *Spring* chart on page 22.

Magnitudes
Measure of Star Brightness

Brightest ○ **0 to –1**
Bright ○ **2nd to 1st**
Average ○ **4th to 3rd**
Faint ∘ **5th**

LEO MINOR

URSA MAJOR

CANES VENATICI

Merak BIG DIPPER *Phad*
Dubhe *Alioth* *Alkaid*
Megrez *Mizar*

Pollux
Castor

GEMINI

LYNX

Thuban

BOOTES

CORONA BOREALIS

This part of the chart attaches to the top of the *Summer* chart on page 24.

SUMMER
This part of the chart attaches to the top of the *Winter* chart on page 20.

AURIGA
Capella

CAMELOPARDALIS

NORTH CELESTIAL POLE

Kochab

URSA MINOR

Polaris
North Star

DRACO

Etamin

HERCULES

WINTER

PERSEUS
Mirphak
Algol

CASSIOPEIA

CEPHEUS

Calph

LYRA *Vega*

Note
All of the stars in this chart are visible from the northern hemisphere.
Some of these stars can be visible from the southern hemisphere.

TRIANGULUM

ANDROMEDA
Mirach

Deneb

CYGNUS

LACERTA

Using this Star Chart

This star chart can be used alone to identify the north circumpolar stars or it can be used in conjunction with the four seasonal charts on pages 18, 20, 22 and 24.

If you use this chart alone, rotate it to the indicated season, then locate the Big Dipper first because it is easiest to see.

If you are using this chart with the others, make sure you match the correct side of the chart as indicated next to each season.

This part of the chart attaches to the top of the **Autumn** chart on page 22.

SPRING

STAND DUE NORTH when looking for these constellations and stars. Start by matching the brightest stars on the chart with those in the sky.
Turn the book for the correct season and orientation.

LEARNING NOTE: The stars in the north are a good starting place for learning constellations because this set of stars is visible year round. Also, the planets are never in this area so they won't cause any confusion.

Size Guide

At an arm's length...

...the width of a fist spans the Big Dipper's bowl.

...the length of the Big Dipper is greater than the spread of your hand.

Stars in the North

The north circumpolar stars are those stars which circle around *Polaris* and never dip below the horizon. In the northern hemisphere, any star at your location that is positioned between *Polaris* and the distance to the horizon is called circumpolar. This creates a large circle of stars that never rise or set. This circle of stars changes with your location on Earth. More stars become circumpolar as you move closer to a pole. At the north pole, all the stars in the sky are circumpolar with *Polaris* directly overhead. Here, the stars nearest the horizon circle the sky in big circles whereas those closest to *Polaris* make little circles. There are no circumpolar stars at the equator because the poles are at the horizon so all the stars rise in the east and set in the west.

Greek lore

URSA MAJOR, the Big Bear, is the princess Callisto, and URSA MINOR, the Little Bear, is her son Arcas. Jupiter, the king of the gods, fell in love with the beautiful Callisto, but his wife Juno became jealous and turned Callisto into a bear roaming the forest. Arcas, while hunting, was about to unknowingly kill his mother so Jupiter intervened, turned him into a bear and sent both to the heavens for the trouble he caused them.

CEPHEUS and CASSIOPEIA were the king and queen of the African country Ethiopia. Cassiopeia bragged that she and her daughter ANDROMEDA were more beautiful than Neptune's mermaids. This enraged Neptune so much that he banished father, mother and daughter to the heavens.

DRACO the Dragon was thrown to the frigid north by the goddess of wisdom, Minerva, during an early war between all the gods.

CAMELOPARDALIS the Giraffe, LACERTA the Lizard and LYNX, a wildcat are constellation made up of faint stars that do not have any lore associated with them because they were added in the 1600s.

Sky notes

The most recognizable northern constellation is actually just a part of the constellation URSA MAJOR. We call it the "Big Dipper." The Big Dipper is very easy to identify because its stars are bright. And, for those living above 40° north latitude in the United States, it is always in the night sky.

On the opposite side of *Polaris* from the Big Dipper is CASSIOPEIA. The Milky Way Band passes right through her. She can resemble a "M" or "W" depending on her position in the sky.

The Big Dipper is easily the most recognized constellation-pattern in the sky. However, many wonder about the Little Dipper because they can't see it. The North Star, *Polaris* is bright and easy to find, but most of the other stars that make up this constellation are faint and can only be seen easily in dark skies.

DRACO wraps around the Little Dipper, positioned as if it had in fact been flung into the sky. Its stars are easier to see than those of the Little Dipper.

The "roof" star of CEPHEUS lies between CASSIOPEIA and *Polaris,* which makes it a good starting point to find the rest of this house-shaped constellation.

Distances & Brightness of Stars

NAME	DISTANCE*	MAGNITUDE
Alioth	81 light years	1¾
Alkaid	101 light years	1¾
Caph	54 light years	2⅓
Dubhe	124 light years	1¾
Etamin	148 light years	2¼
Kochab	126 light years	2
Megrez	81 light years	3⅓
Merak	79 light years	2⅓
Mirphak	592 light years	1¾
Mizar	78 light years	2¼
Phad	84 light years	2½
Polaris	316 light years	2
Thuban	310 light years	4

*One light year is equal to 6 trillion (6,000,000,000,000) miles.

Spring Stars facing South

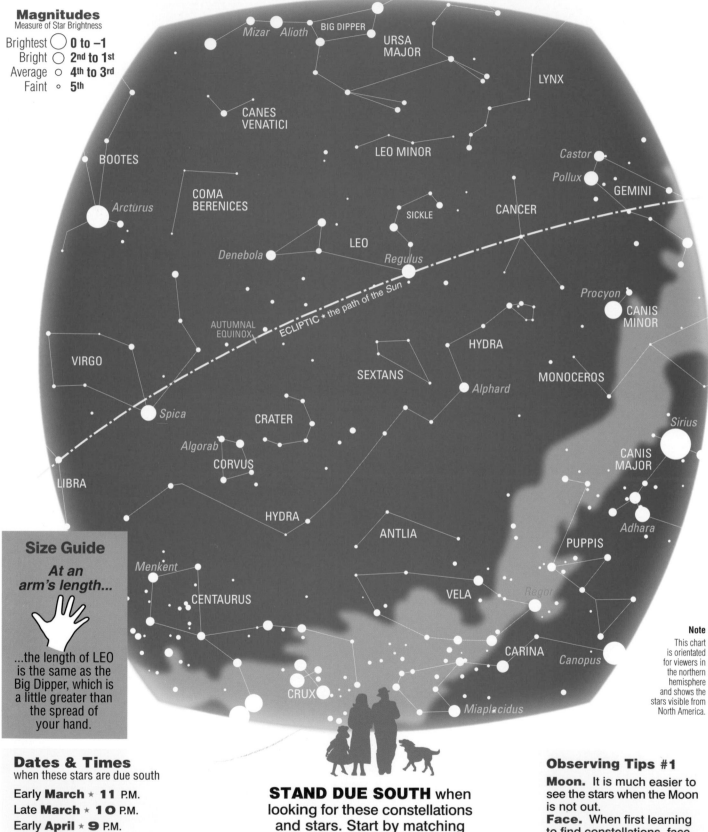

Magnitudes
Measure of Star Brightness

Brightest	◯	**0 to −1**
Bright	◯	**2nd to 1st**
Average	∘	**4th to 3rd**
Faint	·	**5th**

Mizar · Alioth · BIG DIPPER
URSA MAJOR
LYNX
CANES VENATICI
LEO MINOR
Castor
Pollux
GEMINI
BOOTES
COMA BERENICES
SICKLE
CANCER
Arcturus
LEO
CANIS MINOR
Denebola
Regulus
Procyon
AUTUMNAL EQUINOX
ECLIPTIC ★ the path of the Sun
VIRGO
HYDRA
MONOCEROS
SEXTANS
Spica
Alphard
CRATER
Sirius
Algorab
CANIS MAJOR
CORVUS
LIBRA
HYDRA
ANTLIA
Adhara
PUPPIS
Menkent
VELA
Regor
CENTAURUS
CARINA
Canopus
CRUX
Miaplacidus

Size Guide

At an arm's length...

...the length of LEO is the same as the Big Dipper, which is a little greater than the spread of your hand.

Note
This chart is orientated for viewers in the northern hemisphere and shows the stars visible from North America.

Dates & Times
when these stars are due south

Early **March** ★ 11 P.M.
Late **March** ★ 10 P.M.
Early **April** ★ 9 P.M.
Late **April** ★ 8 P.M.
Early **May** ★ 7 P.M.
Late **May** ★ 6 P.M.

STAND DUE SOUTH when looking for these constellations and stars. Start by matching the brightest stars on the chart with those in the sky.

Observing Tips #1

Moon. It is much easier to see the stars when the Moon is not out.
Face. When first learning to find constellations, face either *due* north or south because most star charts are orientated best for these directions.

18

Spring Stars

The spring stars usher in the growth of plants and flourishing of animals. At this time of the year, the constellation VIRGO, often associated with the growing season, rises in the eastern evening sky. Tradition has it that when VIRGO is in the night sky, crops grow, but when she is no longer visible at the end of September, the growing season has ended.

Spring officially begins around March 21. This date can vary by a day or two because of the extra day from leap years. If, on this day, the stars could be seen during the daytime, the *Sun* would be in PISCES at the spot where the ecliptic intersects the projection of the equator onto the sky — a point we call the vernal equinox (see page 13 and star chart on page 22). As spring progresses, the *Sun* gets higher and higher in the sky at noon.

Spring brings warmer days and nights making it easier to stay out longer and enjoy the stars. This is in contrast to the frigid winter nights where we long for nothing less than a blazing fire after just a quick bought outdoors. For many in the U.S. at this time of the year, the *Sun* sets between 7:00 P.M. and 8:00 P.M. and the skies are dark enough to observe the constellations about 60 to 90 minutes later.

Greek lore

There are few stories about LEO the Lion. The most common is that he was the ferocious Nemean Lion from the Moon. Hercules later killed him as one of his twelve labors (see page 21). LEO contains the bright star *Regulus* which has always been known as regal or kingly and is associated with the birth of many kings or leaders.

The HYDRA was a monster that had nine heads. Every time Hercules the Strongman chopped one off, two would grow in its place. CANCER the Crab was sent to prevent Hercules from killing the Hydra, but it failed and was instead killed by the Strongman. Hercules succeeded in killing the Hydra by burning each cut neck stub which prevented it from growing back twice.

CORVUS was a bird placed into the sky on Hydra's back by Apollo, the god of Music and Reason, because he was slow in bringing him water and then lying about why he took so long. CRATER represents a container of water always out of reach of CORVUS.

One story about BOOTES is that he was placed amongst the stars by Jupiter in gratitude for inventing the plow.

CENTAURUS was an centaur, a warlike creature that was half man and half horse. CENTAURUS represents Chiron, the wisest and gentlest of his kind, who educated Hercules, Jason the Argonaut and others. SAGITTARIUS is also a centaur.

Sky notes

LEO is positioned prominently in evening spring skies because it is high overhead when you face south. LEO contains the "Sickle," a set of stars shaped like a backwards question mark that has the bright star *Regulus* acting as its period. If you look due north of LEO, you will bump right into the Big Dipper. When you have found the Big Dipper, follow the curve of its handle eastward, for it points right to the very bright star *Arcturus* in BOOTES and if you continue this arc, it leads to the bright star *Spica*, in VIRGO.

BOOTES is made of stars that are fairly bright so its slice-of-pie shape is easy to follow. Magnificent *Arcturus*, the 4th brightest star in the sky, makes up the point of the pie.

Spring marks the only time of the year that the Milky Way Band is least visible because it hugs the northern horizon from east to west.

Distances & Brightness of Stars

NAME	DISTANCE*	MAGNITUDE
Algorab	88 light years	3
Alphard	177 light years	2
Denebola	36 light years	2⅛
Regulus	77 light years	1⅓
Spica	262 light years	1

*One light year is equal to 6 trillion (6,000,000,000,000) miles.

Summer Stars facing South

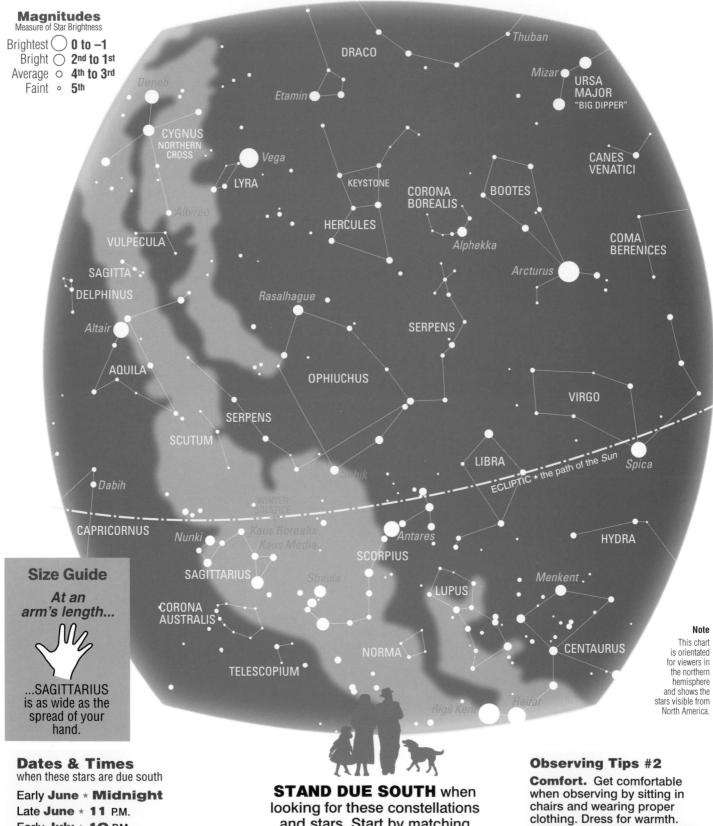

Magnitudes
Measure of Star Brightness

Brightest ◯ 0 to –1
Bright ◯ 2nd to 1st
Average ○ 4th to 3rd
Faint ○ 5th

DRACO

Thuban

Mizar

URSA MAJOR "BIG DIPPER"

Deneb

Etamin

CANES VENATICI

CYGNUS NORTHERN CROSS

Vega

KEYSTONE

CORONA BOREALIS

BOOTES

LYRA

HERCULES

Albireo

VULPECULA

Alphekka

COMA BERENICES

SAGITTA

Arcturus

DELPHINUS

Rasalhague

SERPENS

Altair

OPHIUCHUS

VIRGO

AQUILA

SERPENS

SCUTUM

LIBRA

ECLIPTIC ★ the path of the Sun

Spica

Dabih

WINTER SOLSTICE

HYDRA

CAPRICORNUS

Nunki

Kaus Borealis
Kaus Media

Sabik

Antares

Menkent

SCORPIUS

LUPUS

SAGITTARIUS

Shaula

CORONA AUSTRALIS

NORMA

CENTAURUS

TELESCOPIUM

Rigil Kent

Hadar

Size Guide

At an arm's length...

...SAGITTARIUS is as wide as the spread of your hand.

Note
This chart is orientated for viewers in the northern hemisphere and shows the stars visible from North America.

Dates & Times
when these stars are due south

Early **June** ★ **Midnight**
Late **June** ★ **11** P.M.
Early **July** ★ **10** P.M.
Late **July** ★ **9** P.M.
Early **August** ★ **8** P.M.
Late **August** ★ **7** P.M.

STAND DUE SOUTH when looking for these constellations and stars. Start by matching the brightest stars on the chart with those in the sky.

Observing Tips #2

Comfort. Get comfortable when observing by sitting in chairs and wearing proper clothing. Dress for warmth.
Lights. Turn off outside lights or position yourself away from bright or glaring lights to give your eyes a chance to see the stars better. See more in Tip #3.

Summer Stars

Summer is associated with the appreciation and pause of growth that spring ushered in just months earlier. It is also the hottest time of the year in the northern hemisphere. There is an old saying, "The Dog Days of Summer," which refers to the long hot days that summer brings. However, the origin of this phrase has to do with the dog star, *Sirius*, which rises with the *Sun* during this time of the year. While we bask in the heat of this season, it is difficult to imagine that those living in the southern hemisphere are experiencing frigid winter!

Summer officially begins around June 21 and if, at this time, you could see the stars during the day, the *Sun* would be in TAURUS at the highest northerly point it can reach on the ecliptic. We call this point the Summer Solstice (see star chart on page 24). All those living along the Tropic of Cancer, which is latitude 23½° N and is marked on globes, will see the *Sun* at the *very* top of the sky at noon. All others in the northern hemisphere will experience the *Sun* at the highest it gets in the sky at noon.

Summer has the warmest days and nights, allowing for the most comfortable and extended viewing of the stars. However, it also brings mosquitoes and other annoying bugs that can disturb your viewing tranquility. For many in the U.S., the *Sun* sets between 8:00 P.M. and 9:00 P.M. and the skies are dark enough to observe the constellations about 60 to 90 minutes later.

Greek lore

High up in the sky at this time of the year is HERCULES the Strongman. This constellation pales in comparison to others because it does not contain any bright stars. However, Hercules probably has more stories written about him than any other mythological figure. At one point in his life, Hercules had to decide between two paths: a fun, easy going life or one of virtue but laden with hardships. He chose virtue and was immediately tested with twelve challenges or labors that he successfully passed.

OPHIUCHUS the Doctor, Snake Bearer or Healer used his knowledge to help people in sickness. He learned to make a powerful medicine by watching a snake use a herb for healing.

CYGNUS was changed to a Swan and placed into the heavens by Jupiter for helping locate Phaethon, the son of Helios, who had died by falling from the chariot that pulls the *Sun* across the sky each day.

SCORPIUS the Scorpion slips out from a dark crevice of the Milky Way Band to bite ORION who is healed by Ophiuchus.

SAGITTARIUS the Archer represents the common centaur and its warlike nature. The other centaur, CENTAURUS was kind and gentle.

Sky notes

The famous "Summer Triangle" is formed by the stars *Vega* in LYRA, *Deneb* in CYGNUS and *Altair* in AQUILA. This prominent trio is overhead for much of the summer. CYGNUS is best known and recognized as the Northern Cross.

The Milky Way Band is at its best during this time of the year. Its thickest and brightest part shoots out of the southern horizon, upward from between SCORPIUS and SAGITTARIUS through CYGNUS and on to CASSIOPEIA. The direction to the center of our Milky Way Galaxy lies between SCORPIUS and SAGITTARIUS. This is a good time of the year to take binoculars and explore the band for clumps of stars and other interesting objects.

Distances & Brightness of Stars

NAME	DISTANCE*	MAGNITUDE
Albireo	385 light years	3⅓
Alphekka	75 light years	2¼
Altair	17 light years	¾
Antares	604 light years	1
Arcturus	37 light years	0
Deneb	1467 light years	1¼
Nunki	224 light years	2
Rasalhague	47 light years	2
Sabik	84 light years	2½
Vega	25 light years	0

*One light year is equal to 6 trillion (6,000,000,000,000) miles.

Autumn Stars facing South

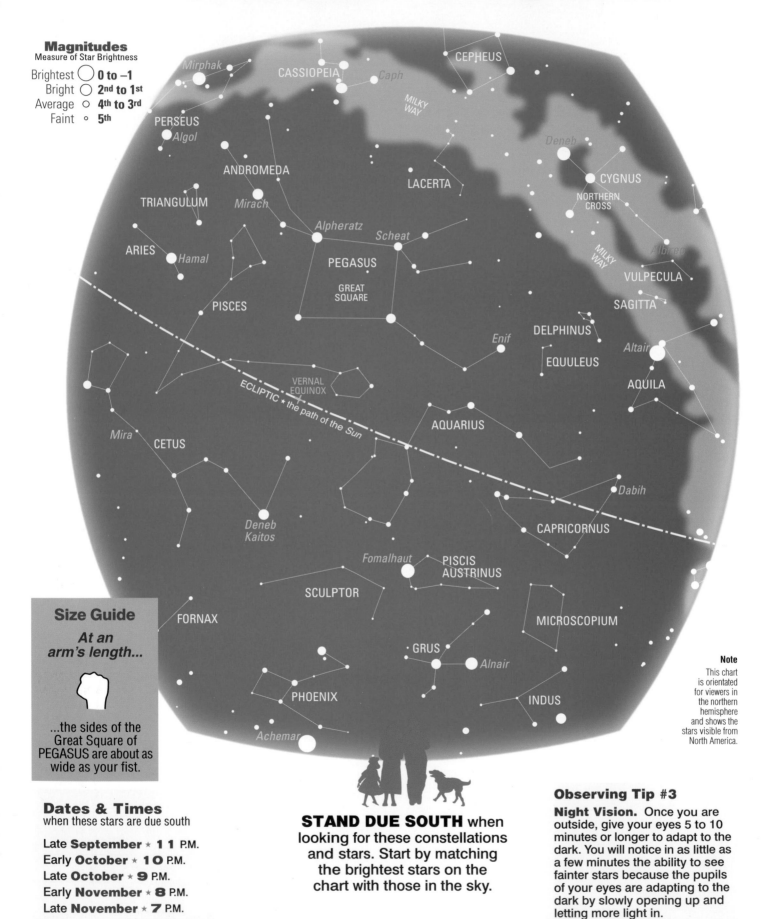

Magnitudes
Measure of Star Brightness

Brightest ◯ **0 to –1**
Bright ◯ **2nd to 1st**
Average ○ **4th to 3rd**
Faint ∘ **5th**

Size Guide

At an arm's length...

...the sides of the Great Square of **PEGASUS** are about as wide as your fist.

Dates & Times
when these stars are due south

Late **September** ★ **11** P.M.
Early **October** ★ **10** P.M.
Late **October** ★ **9** P.M.
Early **November** ★ **8** P.M.
Late **November** ★ **7** P.M.

STAND DUE SOUTH when looking for these constellations and stars. Start by matching the brightest stars on the chart with those in the sky.

Note
This chart is oriented for viewers in the northern hemisphere and shows the stars visible from North America.

Observing Tip #3

Night Vision. Once you are outside, give your eyes 5 to 10 minutes or longer to adapt to the dark. You will notice in as little as a few minutes the ability to see fainter stars because the pupils of your eyes are adapting to the dark by slowly opening up and letting more light in.

Autumn Stars

Autumn brings cooler air and longer nights than summer. The pesky insects have subsided by this time of the year, so observing the stars often becomes more enjoyable than when it was warmer.

Autumn officially begins around September 23. If the stars could be seen during the day at this time, the *Sun* would be in VIRGO, exactly on the celestial equator at a point in the sky that we call the Autumnal Equinox (see page 13 and the star chart on page 18).

At this time of the year and for many in the U.S., the *Sun* sets between 5:30 P.M. and 8:00 P.M. with the skies becoming dark enough to observe the constellations 60 to 90 minutes later.

Greek lore

PEGASUS, a wild and swift Winged Horse was tamed after Athena, the goddess of Victory, gave Bellerophon, a horse handler, the golden bridle to harness the animal. Bellerophon did many great deeds with the help of Pegasus and this eventually led to him becoming a king. However, after many years had passed, he started to believe that he was equal to any god and had Pegasus fly him to Olympus, the home of the gods. Now, mortals are not allowed on the mountain of Olympus so Pegasus bolted before their arrival, throwing Bellerophon to Earth where he became an unknown beggar. Pegasus eventually became the deliverer of Jupiter's thunder and lightening.

AQUARIUS is the Water Carrier who, among other things, poured the water that caused a great flood that killed all but one man and women.

CAPRICORNUS the Seagoat represents the half-transformed body of Pan, the god of Nature. When Pan was on Earth, he often took the form of a goat. One time when he was in this goat body, he got scared by the sudden appearance of the terrible demon called Typhon. Since Typhon took him by surprise, Pan only had time to partially change to a fish before he jumped into the sea to escape Typhon. In the meantime, Typhon had literally torn Jupiter apart and Pan, seeing this carnage, cried out for help. Afterward, Jupiter placed him in the heavens to honor him for his assistance. The word "panic" comes from this story.

PISCES represent two fishes tied together by a long line so they don't get lost from each other. They are the gods Venus and Cupid who turned themselves into fish and jumped into the sea to escape the terrible Typhon.

CETUS, the Sea Monster or Whale, had its head cut off by Perseus when he rescued Andromeda, the daughter of Cepheus and Cassiopeia.

Sky notes

PEGASUS is one of the brightest autumn constellations and is positioned high in the southern sky. Four of its stars form a giant square, called The Great Square, which help to identify it. This horse is the only mythological character that appears to be drawn upside down in comparison to other figures (check out the left chart on the bottom of page 11).

Many of the constellations that surround PEGASUS are water-related. They are CAPRICORNUS, AQUARIUS, CETUS and PISCES. These constellations consist of fainter stars that are hard to see unless you have dark skies. They are also difficult to recognize because their patterns are not easy to follow.

Distances & Brightness of Stars

NAME	DISTANCE*	MAGNITUDE
Alpheratz	97 light years	2
Alnair	101 light years	1¾
Dabih	344 light years	3
Deneb Kaitos	96 light years	2
Enif	672 light years	2⅜
Fomalhaut	25 light years	1⅕
Hamal	66 light years	2
Mirach	199 light years	2
Scheat	199 light years	2½

*One light year is equal to 6 trillion (6,000,000,000,000) miles.

Winter Stars facing South

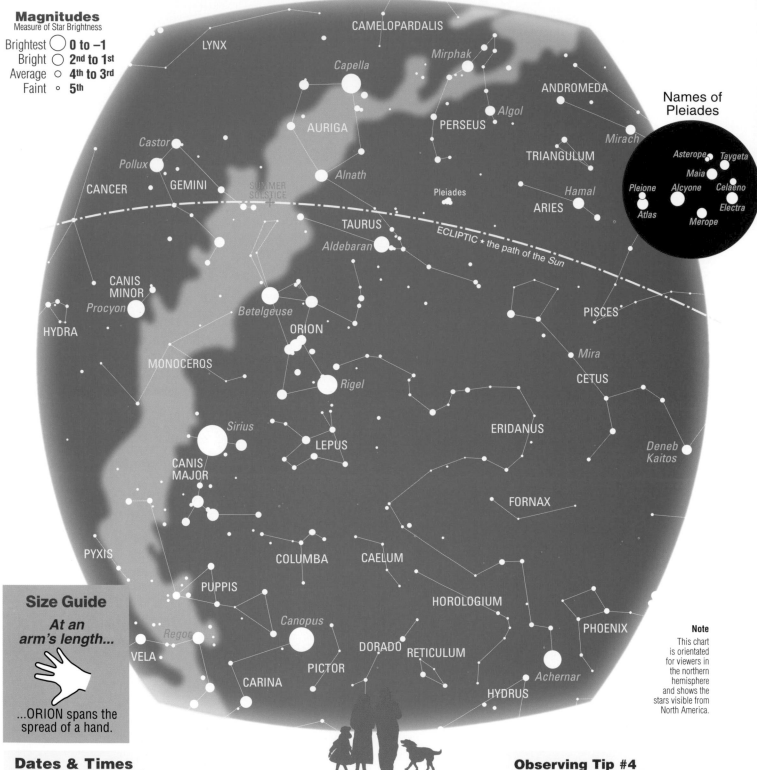

Magnitudes
Measure of Star Brightness

Brightest ⬭ **0 to −1**
Bright ◯ **2nd to 1st**
Average ○ **4th to 3rd**
Faint ∘ **5th**

LYNX
CAMELOPARDALIS
Capella
Mirphak
AURIGA
Algol
PERSEUS
ANDROMEDA
Castor
Pollux
GEMINI
Alnath
Mirach
TRIANGULUM
CANCER
SUMMER SOLSTICE
Pleiades
Hamal
ARIES
TAURUS
Aldebaran
ECLIPTIC ★ the path of the Sun
CANIS MINOR
Procyon
Betelgeuse
ORION
PISCES
HYDRA
MONOCEROS
Mira
CETUS
Rigel
Sirius
LEPUS
ERIDANUS
CANIS MAJOR
Deneb Kaitos
FORNAX
PYXIS
COLUMBA
CAELUM
Regor
VELA
PUPPIS
HOROLOGIUM
PHOENIX
Canopus
DORADO
RETICULUM
Achernar
CARINA
PICTOR
HYDRUS

Names of Pleiades

Asterope *Taygeta*
Maia
Pleione *Alcyone* *Celaeno*
Atlas *Electra*
Merope

Note
This chart is orientated for viewers in the northern hemisphere and shows the stars visible from North America.

Size Guide

At an arm's length...

...ORION spans the spread of a hand.

Dates & Times
when these stars are due south

Early **December** ★ **Midnight**
Late **December** ★ **11** P.M.
Early **January** ★ **10** P.M.
Late **January** ★ **9** P.M.
Early **February** ★ **8** P.M.
Late **February** ★ **7** P.M.

STAND DUE SOUTH when looking for these constellations and stars. Start by matching the brightest stars on the chart with those in the sky.

Observing Tip #4

Planet Confusion. The planets Jupiter, Venus, Saturn and Mars are bright and sometimes brighter than the brightest stars. This may cause some confusion when first learning the constellations. The planets are only visible when facing south and are alway very close to the ecliptic.

Winter Stars

Winter brings cold, long nights. For many of us, it is dark enough at 7:00 P.M. to go outside and look at the stars. However, we tend not to stay out too long because of frigid temperatures and accompanying wind.

Winter officially begins around December 22 and if you could see the stars during the day at this time, the *Sun* would be in SAGITTARIUS at one of two points on the ecliptic called a solstice. In the northern hemisphere, we call this solstice the Winter Solstice (see star chart on page 20). On this day, the *Sun* has reached its southernmost point on the ecliptic. All those living along the Tropic of Capricorn, which is latitude 23½° south and is marked on globes, will see the *Sun* at the *very* top of the sky at noon. Those of us in the northern hemisphere will experience the *Sun* at its lowest noon position.

For most of the United States, the *Sun* sets between 4:30 P.M. and 6:30 P.M. with the sky becoming dark enough to observe stars just 60 to 90 minutes later.

Greek lore

ORION the Hunter has his Hunting Dog, CANIS MAJOR at his heels and LEPUS a Rabbit at his feet. The magical Unicorn, MONOCEROS, the ultimate prize of any hunter is behind him. Orion battles TAURUS the Bull, representing his cleansing of wild beasts from the island of Hyria, a requested deed by its king for the hand of his beautiful daughter in marriage. The king reneged on his promise and burned Orion's eyes out so he could not find his daughter. In order to get his eyesight restored, Orion had to search out the first rays of morning light, just when the *Sun* is pulled into the sky by Helios and his chariot. On his journey to seek Helios, Orion kept a boy cyclops, a one-eyed creature, on his shoulder to help him with directions.

GEMINI the Twins are the war heroes Castor and Pollux; Pollux was immortal and Castor was not. Eventually Castor was killed so Pollux asked Jupiter for death so that he could be with his twin. But immortals cannot be killed so Jupiter allowed him to alternate living one day with the gods and the next in Hades with this brother. Thus the stars, *Castor* and *Pollux* take turns rising and setting in the sky.

The Pleiades or Seven Sisters are not far from Orion. One story has it that Orion liked the sisters but their father Atlas disapproved so the sisters were placed in the sky out of Orion's reach, escaping him by forever rising before him.

Sky notes

The winter sky has the greatest number of bright stars. Next to the Big Dipper, ORION is one of the most recognized constellations in the sky because its bright stars form a very striking pattern. Many people see its three prominent belt stars and wonder what they are. These stars point downward to the brightest star in the whole sky, *Sirius*.

The three stars, *Sirius*, *Procyon* and *Betelgeuse* make up what is called the "Winter Triangle."

If you have very good eyes, you might be able to count seven or even eight stars of the over 100 stars that make up the Pleiades, however, most of us can only count six! The story goes that the seventh sister cries which blurs her brightness and makes her hard to see.

Distances & Brightness of Stars

NAME	DISTANCE*	MAGNITUDE
Aldebaran	65 light years	⅞
Algol	93 light years	2⅛ to 3⅜ **
Alnath	131 light years	1⅝
Betelgeuse	522 light years	½
Capella	42 light years	0
Castor	52 light years	1½
Mira	418 light years	2 to 10 **
Pollux	34 light years	1⅕
Procyon	11 light years	½
Rigel	773 light years	⅕
Sirius	9 light years	−1½

*One light year is equal to 6 trillion (6,000,000,000,000) miles.
**These stars vary in brightness over time.

South Circumpolar Stars

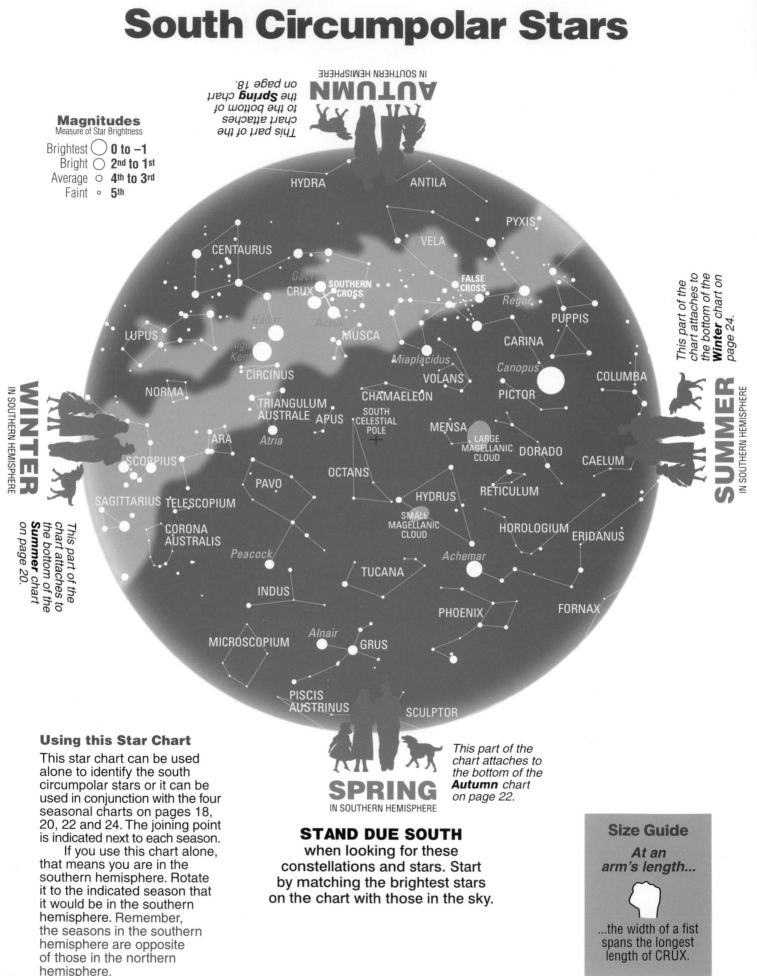

Magnitudes
Measure of Star Brightness

Brightest ◯ **0 to −1**
Bright ◯ **2nd to 1st**
Average ○ **4th to 3rd**
Faint · **5th**

AUTUMN IN SOUTHERN HEMISPHERE

This part of the chart attaches to the bottom of the Spring chart on page 18.

HYDRA

ANTILA

PYXIS

VELA

CENTAURUS

FALSE CROSS

Gacrux
CRUX
SOUTHERN CROSS

Regor

PUPPIS

Hadar
Acrux

CARINA

LUPUS

Rigil Kent

MUSCA

Miaplacidus

Canopus

COLUMBA

CIRCINUS

VOLANS

PICTOR

NORMA

CHAMAELEON

TRIANGULUM AUSTRALE
APUS

SOUTH CELESTIAL POLE

MENSA

ARA

Atria

LARGE MAGELLANIC CLOUD

DORADO

CAELUM

SCORPIUS

PAVO

OCTANS

HYDRUS

RETICULUM

SAGITTARIUS TELESCOPIUM

SMALL MAGELLANIC CLOUD

HOROLOGIUM

ERIDANUS

CORONA AUSTRALIS

Peacock

Achemar

INDUS

TUCANA

PHOENIX

FORNAX

MICROSCOPIUM

Alnair
GRUS

PISCIS AUSTRINUS

SCULPTOR

This part of the chart attaches to the bottom of the Winter chart on page 24.

SUMMER IN SOUTHERN HEMISPHERE

WINTER IN SOUTHERN HEMISPHERE

This part of the chart attaches to the bottom of the Summer chart on page 20.

SPRING
IN SOUTHERN HEMISPHERE

This part of the chart attaches to the bottom of the Autumn chart on page 22.

Using this Star Chart

This star chart can be used alone to identify the south circumpolar stars or it can be used in conjunction with the four seasonal charts on pages 18, 20, 22 and 24. The joining point is indicated next to each season.

If you use this chart alone, that means you are in the southern hemisphere. Rotate it to the indicated season that it would be in the southern hemisphere. Remember, the seasons in the southern hemisphere are opposite of those in the northern hemisphere.

STAND DUE SOUTH
when looking for these constellations and stars. Start by matching the brightest stars on the chart with those in the sky.

Size Guide

At an arm's length...

...the width of a fist spans the longest length of CRUX.

26

Stars in the South

The south circumpolar stars are those stars which circle around the South Celestial Pole and never dip below the horizon. In the southern hemisphere, any star that is positioned between this point and the distance to the horizon is called circumpolar. This creates a large circle of stars that never rise or set. Like with the north circumpolar stars, the size of this circle of stars changes with the latitude of your location on Earth.

No *Polaris* for the South Pole

The Earth's axis points directly to the North Celestial Pole in the northern hemisphere and to the South Celestial Pole in the southern hemisphere. We are fortunate to be alive in a time when *Polaris* is very close to the North Celestial Pole, making it easy to find this point in the sky. However, there is no bright star near the South Celestial Pole which makes it more difficult to find this point in the southern hemisphere skies. Some people use the longest dimension of the constellation CRUX to get close to the South Celestial Pole. If you extend this distance 3½ times, you get close to the South Celestial Pole.

Greek lore

Greece is at about the same latitude as the state of New York. If you live at this latitude on Earth, you cannot see many of the stars in the southern hemisphere. Since this is the case, there is no Greek lore for the most southern of these stars because the ancient Greeks could not see them.

The most notable "lower" constellations with Greek lore are VELA, PUPPIS, CARINA, CENTAURUS and PHOENIX. Vela, Puppis and Carina represent the ship *Argo* sailed by Jason the Argonaut. Vela is the sail, Puppis its stern and Carina its keel. As a boy, Jason was taught by the wise centaur, Chiron and as captain of the *Argo*, he went on many adventures that eventually led him to the Golden Fleece.

Modern names

Most of the constellations of the southern hemisphere are made of fairly faint stars. Some were constructed by a Dutch explorer in the early 1600s and the rest by a Frenchman in the 1750s. They named most of these after either animals or instruments.

Sky notes

Rigel Kent (also written as *Rigel Kentaurus*) is more commonly called *Alpha Centauri*, and is the closest, visible star to us at just about 4 light years away.

There are two Milky Way type clouds "down under" that are detached from the main band. These are called the Large and Small Magellanic Clouds. They are not part of our Milky Way Galaxy but represent small dwarf galaxies that are companions to our galaxy.

Regor is not a particularly bright star but is actually four separate stars that can be seen in binoculars or with a small telescope.

The Southern Cross or CRUX is a favorite object to view when in the southern hemisphere. There is also a false cross, made up of stars in VELA and CARINA that is sometimes confused with the true Southern Cross. CRUX was once a part of CENTAURUS but was broken off by a Frenchman in the 1600s.

Distances & Brightness of Stars

NAME	DISTANCE*	MAGNITUDE
Acrux	321 light years	½
Achemar	144 light years	0¼
Alnair	101 light years	1¾
Atria	415 light years	2
Canopus	313 light years	–⅝
Gacrux	88 light years	1⅝
Hadar	526 light years	⅝
Peacock	183 light years	2
Miaplacidus	111 light years	1⅝
Regor	840 light years	1¾
Rigel Kent	4 light years	1/7

*One light year is equal to 6 trillion (6,000,000,000,000) miles.

Wandering Stars

The stars in the sky are fixed in patterns that we call constellations. However, did you know that there are several stars that move about, wandering through the others?

Ancient observers

For thousands of years, wise people studied the heavens in hopes of unraveling its mysteries. All the time they looked up, they paid special attention to anything new and also to anything that moved. So they carefully watched five stars that did not stay in place but wandered among the others. Two of these stars always stayed close to the rising or setting *Sun*. The remaining three acted a little differently because they could be visible all night long. Normally, these stars moved slightly eastward each night, however, sometimes they would turn and move in the opposite direction for a while before resuming their normal courses. And, there was something even stranger than their movement. Each of these wandering stars changed in brightness!

The ancients did not understand why these five stars did not behave like the rest. Since it was a complete mystery, they named each of them and kept records of their movement. Today, we collectively call these wandering stars by the Greek word for "wanderer," which is "planet." The names given to the earliest known naked-eye wanderers were Mercury, Venus, Mars, Jupiter and Saturn.

The Planets

Mercury and Venus orbit inside Earth's orbit, so they never stray far from the *Sun*. These two planets can appear on the east or west side of the *Sun* depending on where they are in their orbits. This makes them visible for a short time either before sunrise or after sunset. Most people never see Mercury in the sky because its orbit is so close to the *Sun* that it is up for just a short time before sunrise or after sunset.

Sometimes the planets get bunched up in the sky. When two or more planets are relatively close, they are said to be in conjunction. This picture was taken shortly after sunset on May 5, 2002 and shows all five naked-eye planets. The yellow arrow points to a triangle where Mars is the top star, Saturn the left corner star and Venus the bright, right corner star. Mercury is indicated by the pink arrow, Jupiter by the orange arrow and the star *Betelgeuse* by the red arrow.

The orbits of Mars, Jupiter and Saturn are outside Earth's orbit so these planets can often be seen throughout the night. Viewing them is not tied to the rising or setting *Sun*. Uranus, Neptune and Pluto orbit beyond Saturn and were not known to the ancients.

Although Uranus is just visible to the naked eye, it is indistingusiable among the other numerous fainter stars. Neptune requires a small telescope to see while Pluto requires a fairly large telescope, 12-inches or more in diameter to see.

Forward and backwards

All of the planets in our solar system revolve around the *Sun* in the same direction as Earth, which, if you looked down at the north pole, is counterclockwise. It is this counterclockwise movement that makes the planets slowly move eastward through the constellations. The closer a planet is to the *Sun*, the faster it orbits the *Sun* and the faster it moves through the night sky.

Although the planets move eastward through the constellations, regularly the planets Mars through Pluto loop and move backwards or westward in the sky before resuming their normal eastward courses. At these times they *appear* to be traveling backwards but in reality, they are *not* looping or moving westward. These motions are illusions produced by a faster orbiting Earth moving "past" a slower orbiting planet. It is the same effect that happens with a passing car. Both vehicles are moving in the same direction but the slower vehicle appears to be moving backwards when passed. This apparent backwards motion is called retrograde motion.

Brightness

A planet changes in brightness as its distance from Earth changes. Since all of the planets including Earth are in motion around the *Sun*, the distances to each other are constantly changing. For the most part, the closer a planet is to Earth, the brighter it will appear in the night sky. Venus is the brightest planet in the night sky and always outshines any star, including *Sirius*. At its brightest, it is 18 times brighter than *Sirius*. Jupiter, the largest planet in the solar system, is consistently the brightest planet in the sky and also outshines *Sirius*. It can shine all night long whereas Venus is only visible for a short time around the rising and setting *Sun*. Generally, Mars gets lost with most other average brightness stars but about every two years when it gets very close to Earth, it becomes very bright and red for a few months.

Morning & evening stars

The "Morning Star" or "Evening Star" gener-

ally refers to Venus but these terms can also apply to Mercury or any of the other naked-eye planets. Generally, when the very bright and noticeable Venus appears in the western sky after sunset, we call it the Evening Star. We call it the Morning Star when it appears in the eastern sky before sunrise.

Planets and Zodiac

If you watched the planets over the years, you would also find that their paths through the sky never take them far from the ecliptic, so they stay in the constellations of the zodiac.

LEO
The Lion

"The Sickle"

Denebola

3rd
May 8, 2 B.C.

2nd
Feb. 17, 2 B.C.

1st Sep. 14, 3 B.C.

Regulus

Jupiter's path in sky

4th

Jupiter & Venus are so close together on Jun. 17, 2 B.C. that they appear as a single bright star.

The Star of Bethlehem

What was the star of Bethlehem? No one knows for certain but some scholars think that the Magi or wise men witnessed three close approaches of Jupiter with *Regulus*, then an ending where Jupiter and Venus blended into one star, all within a span of 9 months. To many cultures, *Regulus* was the "regal" star while Jupiter was the king of the planets. What could be more ominous than these two royal bodies coming together? These events were the result of retrograde motion bringing about several conjunctions. The orange line in the illustration shows Jupiter's retrograde motion above *Regulus* (creating a crown) ending in an extremely rare conjunction where two planets overlap (not physically, but from our line of sight). The Magi certainly must have realized that something rare and special was happening, even if it was only an astronomical event. Note: The years for B.C. dates count backward, which is why the 1st approach that happened in 3 B.C. has a year that is greater than the 2nd to 4th events, which happened after the first, but occurred in the year 2 B.C..

Remember, the ecliptic, which is the path of the *Sun* through the sky, really represents the movement and orbit of the Earth around the *Sun*. If the planets orbited the *Sun* in the same plane as Earth's orbit, the paths of the planets in the sky would fall right on the ecliptic. But this is not the case. The orbits of the other planets are tilted slightly to Earth's orbit, so their paths in the sky are only close to the ecliptic.

The fact that the naked-eye planets are confined to the constellations of the zodiac is helpful in distinguishing them from stars. For example, if you looked up at GEMINI and saw an extra, very bright star (which would probably be Jupiter) or a fairly bright star (which would be Saturn or Mars) then you would know that this extra star would have to be a planet.

This cone-shaped iron meteorite is an example of an "orientated" meteor that did not tumble during its flight through our atmosphere. Its shape, which resembles the noses of space shuttles, was formed by the air pushing back on its molten surface.

Actual top to bottom height is 2¾ inches.

This South American shaped iron meteorite is a slice from a larger piece. The crisscrossing lines are a crystalline pattern formed from cooling in space. Earth rocks do not show this pattern.

Actual length is 3½ inches.

The indents on this iron meteorite are nicknamed "thumbprints" because your fingers or thumb will fit into them. These depressions formed when parts of the meteorite became molten and were then pushed into bowls by the air as it pierced our atmosphere.

Longest length is actually 1½ inches.

This stony chondrite meteorite is made of spherical particles (silicates) which can be seen as the circles in the part that was cut away. This type of meteorite may represent the oldest type of rock in the solar system.

Longest length is actually 7 inches.

Observing Meteor Showers

The best time to observe meteor showers is from about 10:00 at night to an hour or so before the *Sun* rises in the morning. More meteors are seen at this time because the night side of the Earth is turned toward and thus charging into the path of meteoroid streams. Don't get discouraged if you can't observe them at this time because you will still see meteors earlier in the evening. When observing meteors, you do not have to face any particular direction but it is probably best to lie on your back in a lounge chair and look straight up so you can see more of the sky and therefore more meteors. All the showers generally last a few days, so use the dates as guidelines. A bright Moon will ruin any shower because it whitewashes the sky making it harder to see meteors. Dress warmly to keep comfortable and enjoy the show!

Major Meteor Showers

Shower & (CONSTELLATION)	Date	Hourly Count
Quadrantids* (BOOTES)	**Jan 3**	**60 – 200**
Lyrids (LYRA)	**Apr 22**	**15 – 20+**
Eta **Aquarids** (AQUARIUS)	**May 5**	**60**
Delta **Aquarids** (AQUARIUS)	**Jul 29**	**20**
Perseids (PERSEUS)	**Aug 12**	**120 – 160**
Orionids (ORION)	**Oct 21**	**20**
Taurids (TAURUS)	**Nov 5–13**	**5**
Leonids (LEO)	**Nov 17**	**10**
Geminids (GEMINI)	**Dec 14**	**120**
Ursids (URSA MINOR)	**Dec 22**	**10+**

*The Quadrantids is named after an obsolete constellation recognized in the 1800s.

Shooting Stars

Have you ever seen a shooting star? It is a bright streak in the night sky that lasts only a second but is fun and exciting to see. A shooting star has nothing to do with the stars. It is just a common name for a meteor. The light of a meteor, or shooting star is produced when a rock from space enters our atmosphere, heating up so much that it gives off light.

Meteoroids

The rocks in space that slam into our atmosphere and become meteors are called meteoroids. They orbit the *Sun* like Earth but sometimes their orbits cross ours, causing them to enter the atmosphere at speeds reaching 40 miles per second (144,000 miles per hour). This is so fast that friction with the air causes the rocks to heat up so much, they become molten and give off light. To feel heat produced by friction, quickly and tightly rub the palms of your hands together.

Comet meteors

Most meteors that are seen in the night sky are created by very small rocks, meteoroids that are the size of grains of sand. Many of these sand particles come from comets. Comets are a mixture of ice and sand. When they are far out in the solar system, they look like giant icebergs. But sometimes, their orbits bring them close to the *Sun*. This causes them to warm up, turning the ice to vapor, releasing the trapped sand particles, which can then strike the Earth's atmosphere to become meteors. These sand-size meteoroids totally burn up in the atmosphere and never hit the ground.

Asteroid-belt meteors

The brightest meteors, those that can light up the whole night sky, are created by meteoroids ranging in size from an average rock in your driveway to as big or bigger than a house. These meteoroids are not from comets but are chunks from the asteroid belt that have wandered sunward crossing Earth's path. These meteoroids often survive their journey through the atmosphere and hit the ground. Meteoroids that hit the ground are called meteorites.

This woodcut, which is a carving in wood that is then inked and printed on paper, shows the Leonid storm of November 12, 1799. A storm is a very rare type of meteor shower in which dozens to thousands of meteors fall every *minute*.

Meteorites

On the opposite page are pictures of meteorites, rocks from space that fell to Earth. Meteorites represent the original type of material that formed the Earth, as well as some of the other planets and moons in our solar system.

There are several different types of meteorites, but one of the most popular that is often seen at museums is the iron meteorite which contains a mixture of iron and nickel. There are also stony-type meteorites that are made of silicates, which is the same stuff that common rocks are made of. Chondrites are a class of stony meteorites that are believed to be made of the oldest material in our solar system. They are composed of small round silicate spheres.

Meteor showers

Would you like to see a meteor? On any night, about seven meteors can be seen in an hour. But you will easily miss them if you are not looking in the direction that they fall. You have the best chance of seeing more meteors during meteor showers which happen several times a year. During these times, anywhere from 20 to 200 per hour can be seen. Meteor showers occur when the paths or orbits of comet debris, which consist of sand particles, overlap onto Earth's orbit.

For any shower, if you took all its meteor streaks (the lines or paths made by each of the meteors in the sky) and extended them backwards, you would find that they would all intersect at one spot in the sky. Showers are named after the constellation that this spot falls in.

Glossary

This glossary has been expanded to include terms and concepts that are not in the main body of this book and are offered to provide additional information about the stars. The definitions for many words used in this book can be found on the pages listed in the Index.

Spelling of the names of stars. You will find that the spelling for the names of some stars vary from book to book. This is because many of these names originally came from Arabic, a language that does not use the same letters as our English language. Arabic is very different from English, so when an Arabic word is written in English, the spelling of the word is based on the sound of the Arabic. However, as you have experienced with English words, there are often several letters or letter combinations that can give you the same sound. For this reason, Arabic words that are written in English are often spelled differently because they were spelled by different scholars. For example, *Alphekka* in CORONA BOREALIS is also spelled *Alphecca*.

→ Read

Aldebaran	الدبران	
Alpheratz	سرّة الفرس	
Antares	قلب العقرب	
Betelgeuse	إبط الجوزاء	
Deneb	ذنب الدجاجة	
Rigel	رِجل الجوزاء اليسرى	

The names of these six stars came from Arabic words that are shown to their right. Arabic is one of the few languages that is written and read from right to left. The language consists of 28 letters and is always written in script. There are no capital letters.

Atlas. A collection of maps or charts that is often in book form.

Arabs. The Arabs are people who speak Arabic. Their language and culture started around 800 B.C. arising from nomadic tribes that wandered the area around Saudi Arabia. The tribes became more organized when the prophet Mohammed introduced Islam, the religion of the Arabs, around A.D. 600. From about A.D. 700 to 1400, the Arabs expanded their influence as far as Spain and went on to make significance contributions in literature, philosophy, medicine and mathematics. The word algebra comes from Arabic.

Arc (Angle) Degrees, Arc Minutes and Arc Seconds. *Also see* Protractor. A system of measurement used for angles, based on a circle divided evenly into 360 parts that are called arc degrees. One arc degree is subdivided

into 60 arc minutes and one arc minute is further subdivided into 60 arc seconds. Arc degrees have nothing to do with temperature and arc minutes and arc seconds have nothing to do with time on a clock. Often, the word "arc" is not used when referring to the angular measurements of degrees, minutes and seconds and this can cause confusion. The abbreviation for degrees is (°), for minutes (') and for seconds ("). Example: 123° 15' 32".

Celestial Equator. A "great circle" in the sky that is the projection of Earth's equator onto the celestial sphere. It divides the celestial sphere into two parts, a northern and southern. Some of the constellations that it passes through are ORION (near the three belt stars), VIRGO, OPHIUCHUS, AQUILA and PISCES.

Celestial Sphere. This is an old term that is still used today. The ancients did not know the true nature of the stars and their best guess was that they were some kind of light or fire resting on a giant dome or sphere that surrounded the Earth. To the eyes, all the stars in the sky appear to be the same distance away. This produces the effect that they are on a giant sphere or ball. Today, we use this term to refer to the realm of where the stars reside. But the idea of a celestial sphere has also been useful as a "surface" for creating a coordinate system to indicate the position of celestial objects much like we use globes and latitude and longitude to indicate locations on Earth.

Chart. A chart is a term that is often used to refer to a map of the stars in the sky. It can also refer to a map that indicates the depth and shape of rivers, lakes and oceans.

Chinese. The people that settled and lived in the greater area of China. The Chinese civilization represents one of the oldest and longest continuing cultures in the world. Northern China was first organized by a ruler around 1500 B.C. and it was not until later, about 250 B.C. that the first of many emperors ruled the country. From 200 B.C. to 1300 A.D.,

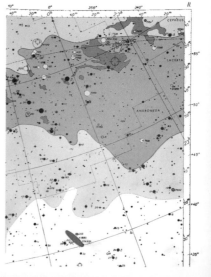

Part of a star chart from an atlas. The 3 black straight lines are lines of Right Ascension and the 3 black curved lines are lines of Declination. You can see how these coordinates are indicated on the top and right sides of the chart. The large blue areas on this chart indicate the Milky Way and the bottom red oval is the Andromeda Galaxy, a compansion galaxy to our Milky Way Galaxy.

the Chinese flourished and made significant contributions in the arts and sciences. They invented the first printing presses, applied the use of magnetic compasses to navigation and developed gunpowder.

Clockwise and Counterclockwise. Clockwise is the circular movement that is in the same direction as the hands on a clock. Counterclockwise is a circular movement opposite the direction the hands on a clock move.

Conjunction. A conjunction is an "event" in the sky when the Moon and a planet, or two or more planets, appear close to one another in the sky (see picture on page 28). In reality, the Moon and planets are not near each other during conjunctions; they just appear close to one another because they lie in the same direction.

Declination. *See* Right Ascension and Declination.

Great Circle. The largest possible circle that can be drawn on the celestial sphere. The celestial equator and ecliptic are great circles. Any circle that passes through both celestial poles would be a great circle.

Greeks. The ancient Greek civilization occupied the surrounding land of the Aegean Sea, which is part of the greater Mediterranean Sea. They settled this area as early as 1900 B.C. Their golden age occurred from 500 B.C. to 323 B.C., the time of Plato and Aristotle. Although the Romans conquered the Greeks around 30 B.C., the Roman's culture was heavily influenced by the Greeks. Much of our modern thinking and way of life has roots in the Greek culture.

Inferior Planets. The planets in our solar system that orbit inside Earth's orbit. This includes Mercury and Venus. *Also see* Superior Planets.

Latitude and Longitude. A pair of coordinates (arc angles) used to indicate the location of any spot on Earth. Examples include: 25° N, 142° E; 78° S, 45° W; 24° N, 0°. The first number of these pairs of numbers is the latitude (with a **N**orth or **S**outh following it) and the second number is longitude (with an **E**ast or **W**est following it). Latitude is an arc angle number between 0° and 90° that indicates your position from the equator to one of the poles on Earth. Latitude 0° is the band of the equator. 90° north

Greenwich (London)

The 8 straight red lines are lines of longitude and the 4 curved red lines are lines of latitude. It was agreed upon at an international conference in 1884 that the 0° longitude would pass through the Royal Observatory at Greenwich, England.

is the north pole and 90° south is the south pole. Latitudes are indicated as either North or South of the equator. On a globe, latitudes are the circles that are parallel to the equator and get smaller the closer they are to the poles. Longitudes lines are north-south half-circles that stretch from pole to pole. They represent an arc angle measurement and are assigned a number between 0° and 180° starting at Greenwich, England, a small town next to London. Locations east of Greenwich are designated East and locations west are designated West. The 180° longitude passes through the middle of the Pacific Ocean. The vertical lines on a map or globe are the longitude lines. The degrees of latitude and longitude are further divided into arc minutes and arc seconds. *See* Arc (Angle) Degrees, Arc Minutes and Arc Seconds.

Light Year. A unit of length based on the distance that light travels in one year. Since light travels at the rate of 186,282 miles per second, in one year's time, it will travel the distance of almost 6 trillion miles (one light year equals 5,874,589,000,000 miles).

Longitude. See Latitude and Longitude.

Map. A map usually refers to drawings of land on Earth.

North (or South) Celestial Pole. The points in the sky that Earth's poles or axes ends point to. Both points are 90° from the celestial equator, just like the north and south poles are 90° from Earth's equator. The star *Polaris* is very close to the north celestial pole but it is not exactly at this point. There is no bright star near the south celestial pole. The north celestial pole is in the constellation URSA MINOR while the south celestial pole is in the constellation OCTANS.

Northern Hemisphere. The part of Earth that lies north or "above" the equator.

Orbit. The path of an object as it revolves around another object. The orbits of the planets are shaped like slightly elongated circles or ovals that are called ellipses.

Protractor. A device used to measure or create angles. The divisions of a protractor are based on a circle divided into 360 equal parts called arc degrees or sometimes just called degrees (don't get this confused with temperature degrees which is a different measurement). Each degree is further subdivided into 60 arc minutes and each arc minute is subdivided into 60 arc seconds. These minutes and seconds are not related to time on a clock. Arc degrees, minutes and seconds are used in astronomy to measure the *angular* separation between stars or span of an object. For example, the Moon and *Sun* appear about the same arc size in the sky. How many arc degrees do you think the

Glossary

A common protractor spans 180° because it represent just one-half of a circle. The numbering goes both ways for ease-of-use in measuing and creating angles. **Below.** Top of the protractor. If you projected the divisions of a protractor onto the sky, you would find that the Moon or *Sun* spans only ½ of an arc degree.

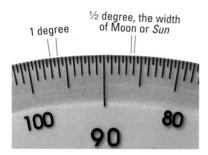

1 degree

½ degree, the width of Moon or *Sun*

diameter of the Moon or *Sun* spans in the sky? See the caption to the left for the answer.

Why is a circle divided into 360 divisions instead of 100? This was something that was decided long ago because it is easier to evenly divide commonly used numbers into 360 than 100. For example, the numbers 1, 2, 3, 4, 5, 6, 8, 9, 10, 12, 15, 18 and others will evenly divide into 360, which provides many choices to divide up a circle in equal parts. Now, how many of these numbers listed will divide into 100? That is the reason why 100 was not used.

Revolve (Revolution). The words "revolve" and "rotate" are often confused. Revolve means to circle around another object. Our planets revolve, circle or orbit around the *Sun*. See Rotate, to the right.

Right Ascension and Declination. (Read about Latitude and Longitude on page 33 before reading this. Also see the star chart at the bottom of page 32.) Right Ascension and Declination are celestial coordinates, like latitude and longitude, that are used to indicate the position of stars, planets and other objects in the sky. The latitude and longitude coordinate system used for Earth could have been used for the sky but astronomers decided on a different system to take advantage of the fact that the stars circle around the sky once a day.

Right Ascension is akin to longitude. The lines of Right Ascension are half circles that stretch from the north to south celestial poles. There are 24 major divisions of Right Ascension corresponding to the 24 hours on a clock. Each hour of Right Ascension is subdivided into 60 minutes and each minute is further subdivided into 60 seconds. These hours, minutes and seconds *are* related to the time on the clock. The zero hour of Right Ascension starts at the vernal equinox, an intersection of the ecliptic and celestial equator (see chart on page 22).

Declination is very similar to latitude. In fact, Declination uses the same measurement as latitude. 0° Declination starts at the celestial equator and ends with 90° at either celestial pole. Declinations north of the celestial equator are indicated by a plus sign (+),

and those south of the celestial equator are indicated by a minus or negative sign (–).

An example of a pair of celestial coordinates is: 5h 32' 14", +32° 16' 59". The first set of three numbers is the Right Ascension and the second set of three numbers is the Declination. In this system, the minutes and seconds for Right Ascension is a TIME measurement and the minutes and seconds for Declination is an ARC ANGLE measurement.

Mostly, the separation or distance between objects in the sky is measured using the arc angle system, the same system used with protractors. However, Right Ascension is a convenient and useful measurement for determining east/west position and/or movement of heavenly bodies. For example, let's say that you looked up in the sky and noticed that *Sirius* was exactly due south. Now, you also know (because you love astronomy so much that you studied and memorized everything about it) that the star *Spica* is about 6 hours farther east in Right Ascension. This means that *Spica* will appear due south in the sky 6 hours from the time you saw *Sirius* due south.

Rotate (Rotation). The words "rotate" and "revolve" are often confused. To rotate is to spin. Any object that is spinning is rotating. Objects rotate about an axis. *See* Revolve, to the left.

South Celestial Pole. *See* North Celestial Pole.

Southern Hemisphere. The half of Earth that lies south or "below" the equator.

Superior Planets. The planets in our solar system that orbit beyond Earth's orbit. These include Mars, Jupiter, Saturn, Uranus, Neptune and Pluto. *Also see* Inferior Planets.

Twinkling of Planets. Most of the time, you can distinguish a planet from a star because the planets don't twinkle (see twinkling of stars on page 4). The reason the naked-eye planets rarely twinkle is because they actually have a small diameter in our sky compared to the stars. When you look through a telescope, all stars appear as pinpoints but the planets appear as small disks because they are very close to us compared to the stars (remember the stars are as big as our *Sun* but they are very far away). Light that passes through our atmosphere but comes from a small disk does not jump around as much as pinpoint light. An extreme example of this is the Moon. Have you ever seen it twinkle?

Index

Contributors

David H. Levy and Ken Graun

Ken Graun is the author of the first two books in this series, *Our Earth and the Solar System* and *Our Galaxy and the Universe*. He also wrote the popular astronomy field guides, *Touring the Universe* and *What's Out Tonight?* He and David H. Levy are coauthors of several beginner's star charts, including a version translated into Spanish. Ken lectures and is writing more astronomy books for beginners and children.

David H. Levy is an Emmy award-winning author who has written more than 30 books on astronomy. He is the science editor for the weekly *Parade* magazine and contributes articles to several monthly publications. David has discovered 21 comets including Comet Shoemaker-Levy 9 that smashed into Jupiter in 1994. He continues to search for comets, write, lecture and promote science.

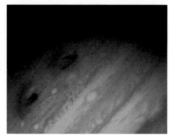

These two dark patches on Jupiter were caused by impacts from Comet Shoemaker-Levy 9.

Special thanks to Barbara McNichol for proofreading and Carolyn Randall for working on the star charts.

Website

VISIT
whatsouttonight.com

Photo Credits

Front cover. Milky Way: SCOTT TUCKER, Pleiades: ANGLO-AUSTRALIAN OBSERVATORY/ROYAL OBSERVATORY EDINBURGH, Taurus the Bull: VISUAL LANGUAGE, All others: KEN GRAUN. *Back cover*. ANGLO-AUSTRALIAN OBSERVATORY/ROYAL OBSERVATORY EDINBURGH. *Page 1*. ANGLO-AUSTRALIAN OBSERVATORY/ROYAL OBSERVATORY EDINBURGH. *Page 3*. KEN GRAUN. *Page 5*. Pillars of Creation: JEFF HESTER AND PAUL SCOWEN (ARIZONA STATE UNIVERSITY) AND NASA, Galaxy: EUROPEAN SOUTHERN OBSERVATORY. *Page 6*. Earths: PLANETARY VISIONS, All others: KEN GRAUN. *Page 6/7*. Pictures/graphics: KEN GRAUN. *Page 10*. VISUAL LANGUAGE. *Page 11*. Top graphic: KEN GRAUN, Bottom pictures: VISUAL LANGUAGE. *Page 12*. Charts: VISUAL LANGUAGE, Earths: PLANETARY VISIONS. *Page 13*. KEN GRAUN. *Page 14*. SCOTT TUCKER. *Page 15*. Photo of Milky Way Band: NASA/COBE/DIRBE, All others: KEN GRAUN. *Pages 16 to 27*. Star Charts: KEN GRAUN and CAROLYN RANDALL. *Pages 28/29*. KEN GRAUN. *Page 30*. KEN GRAUN. *Page 31*. AURA/NOAO/NSF. *Page 32*. Atlas of the Heavens: KEN GRAUN. *Page 33*. DIGITAL WISDOM. *Page 34*. KEN GRAUN. *Page 36*. Top: KEN GRAUN, Jupiter: NASA (STSCI).

What are constellations? Where did they get their names? What is a falling star? What and where is the zodiac? Is the North Star the brightest star in the sky?

Up-to-date answers to these and other questions can be found in this illustrated book about the stars.

Our Constellations and their Stars introduces youngsters to the wonders of astronomy by exploring the very stars they see in the night sky. Learning about them will occur naturally as they examine photographs and drawings, compare facts and follow the explanatory text. There are even star charts to aid in finding and observing every constellation in the sky.

Suitable for...
Ages 8 through 13.
Grades 4 through 7.

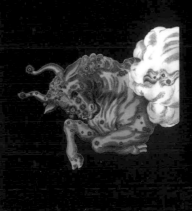

The 88 Constellations of the Heavens

NAME	Pronumciation	Abbreviation	Meaning of Name	Chart Page No.
ANDROMEDA	an-DROM-eh-dah	And	Daughter of Cassiopeia	16, 22, 24
ANTLIA	ANT-lee-ah	Ant	Air Pump	18, 26
APUS	A-pus	Aps	Bird of Paradise	26
AQUARIUS	ah-KWARE-ee-us	Aqr	Water Bearer	22
AQUILA	ah-KWIL-ah	Aql	Eagle	20, 22
ARA	A-rah	Ara	Altar	26
ARIES	AIR-ease	Ari	Ram	22, 24
AURIGA	oh-RYE-gah	Aur	Charioteer	16, 24
BOOTES	BOAT-ease or bo-O-tease	Boo	Herdsman	16, 18, 20
CAELUM	SEE-lum	Cae	Engraving Tool	24, 26
CAMELOPARDALIS	kah-MEL-o-PAR-dah-lis	Cam	Giraffe	16, 24
CANCER	CAN-sir	Cnc	Crab	18, 24
CANES VENATICI	KAY-nez vee-NAT-e-see	CVn	Hunting Dog	16, 18, 20
CANIS MAJOR	KAY-nis MAY-jor	CMa	Big Dog	18, 24
CANIS MINOR	KAY-nis MY-nor	CMi	Little Dog	18, 24
CAPRICORNUS	CAP-pra-corn-us	Cap	Sea Goat	20, 22
CARINA	ka-REE-nah	Car	Ship's Keel	18, 24, 26
CASSIOPEIA	kass-e-o-PEA-ah	Cas	Queen	16, 22
CENTAURUS	sen-TAR-us	Cen	Centaur	18, 20, 26
CEPHEUS	SEE-fee-us	Cep	King	16, 22
CETUS	SEE-tus	Cet	Whale	22, 24
CHAMAELEON	kah-ME-lee-un	Cha	Chameleon	26
CIRCINUS	sir-SEE-nus	Cir	Drawing Compass	26
COLUMBA	koe-LUM-bah	Col	Dove	24, 26
COMA BERENICES	KOE-mah bu-REN-e-sees	Com	Berenice's Hair	18, 20
CORONA AUSTRALIS	koe-ROW-nah os-TRAY-lis	CrA	Southern Crown	20, 26
CORONA BOREALIS	koe-ROW-nah bore-ee-AL-iss	CrB	Northern Crown	20
CORVUS	CORE-vus	Crv	Crow	18
CRATER	KRAY-ter	Crt	Cup	18
CRUX	KRUCKS	Cru	Southern Cross	26
CYGNUS	SIG-nus	Cyg	Swan	16, 20, 22
DELPHINUS	del-FYE-nus	Del	Dolphin	20, 22
DORADO	doe-RAH-doe	Dor	Goldfish	24, 26
DRACO	DRAY-koe	Dra	Dragon	16, 20
EQUULEUS	eh-KWOO-lee-us	Equ	Little Horse	22
ERIDANUS	ee-RID-ah-nus	Eri	River Eridanus	24, 26
FORNAX	FOR-nacks	For	Furnace	22, 24, 26
GEMINI	JEM-ah-nye	Gem	Twins	16, 18, 24
GRUS	GRUS	Gru	Crane	22, 26
HERCULES	HER-cue-leas	Her	Son of Zeus	16, 20
HOROLOGIUM	hore-o-LOW-jee-um	Hor	Clock	24, 26
HYDRA	HI-drah	Hya	Sea Serpent	18, 20, 24. 26
HYDRUS	HI-drus	Hyi	Water Snake	24, 26
INDUS	IN-dus	Ind	Indian	22, 26
LACERTA	lah-SIR-tah	Lac	Lizard	16, 22
LEO	LEE-o	Leo	Lion	18
LEO MINOR	LEE-o MY-nor	LMi	Little Lion	16, 18
LEPUS	LEE-pus	Lep	Hare	24
LIBRA	LEE-brah	Lib	Scales	20
LUPUS	LOO-pus	Lup	Wolf	20, 26
LYNX	LINKS	Lyn	Lynx	16, 18, 24
LYRA	LYE-rah	Lyr	Lyre	16, 20